THE GOSPEL-CENTERED COMMUNITY FOR TEENS

THE
GOSPEL-CENTERED
COMMUNITY
FOR TEENS

Robert H. Thune and Will Walker

STUDY GUIDE WITH LEADER'S NOTES

New
Growth
Press

newgrowthpress.com

New Growth Press, Greensboro, NC 27401
newgrowthpress.com

Cover Design: Faceout Studio, faceoutstudio.com
Interior Typesetting and Ebook: Lisa Parnell, lparnellbookservices.com

ISBN: 978-1-64507-511-0 (paperback)
ISBN: 978-1-64507-512-7 (ebook)

Printed in the United States of America

29 28 27 26 25   1 2 3 4 5

CONTENTS

INTRODUCTION

FROM THE AUTHORS

For over two decades now, we have been involved in forming and leading gospel-centered communities. We started out in campus ministry, and then we applied our experience to the realm of church planting. As our churches matured, and as our own kids grew up, we began to give more attention to the incredible opportunity to help teens experience the gospel together.

One thing we've learned is that without the gospel, community groups will always become unhealthy. Some will become ingrown and self-absorbed. Others will become busy and activist. Either way, they will lose their power to display the glory and grace of God. Only with the gospel at the center can a community become a thriving culture of discipleship, fellowship, and Spirit-empowered mission.

This study is a follow-up to *The Gospel-Centered Life for Teens*. That study focused on personal renewal. This one seeks to apply the same principles to community life. Through a combination of Bible study, reflection, discussion, and application, we want to help your community experience the transforming power of the gospel.

ABOUT THIS STUDY

People often talk about the content of the gospel—the message we must believe to be saved. What often gets overlooked is the fact that we are saved into a community. That is why so much of the Bible is about how to live in community. Believing the gospel means learning to love one another as Christ has loved us.

That is why we wrote *The Gospel-Centered Community for Teens*. This study will deepen your understanding of the gospel and help you apply it to the life of your community.

It's one thing to see the need for gospel-centered community. It's another thing to cultivate it. How do you take a small group, or a youth group, and build a vibrant gospel culture within it? That's where we hope this study will help.

HOW THIS STUDY IS ORGANIZED

The Gospel-Centered Community for Teens contains eight lessons that are grouped into two major sections. The Leader's Guide contains all the information needed to facilitate the group.

Section 1: The Foundation of Gospel-Centered Community

LESSON 1: THE CHALLENGE OF COMMUNITY

We've all felt left out, like we're looking at other people's relationships from the outside with our faces pressed against the window. We long for relationship. But so often it's hard to find, and we're left feeling alone. On the flip side, when we do find relationships and are part of a community, they turn out to be hard—sometimes *really* hard. In this lesson, we'll take a quick look at the landscape of modern relationships.

LESSON 2: THE BACKSTORY

Where did our need for community come from? As human beings we long for relationships that are meaningful—and this longing comes from God himself. God is relational and loving, and he made us in his image. But as we all know, relationships can be a source of pain and frustration. What went wrong? In this lesson we'll explore why we have such a need for relationships, why they're so hard, and why we can have real hope in spite of the hard things.

LESSON 3: HOW DO WE DO CHRISTIAN COMMUNITY?

We've looked at our need for community, the reason why community can be difficult, and the hope we have because of the work of Jesus and the power of the Holy Spirit. But what *is* Christian community? And how does it work? An essential quality of Christian community is *faith expressing itself through love*. This means that faith in all that God has given us through Jesus moves and enables us to love others.

Section 2: The Fruit of Gospel-Centered Community

LESSON 4: A GRACE-FILLED COMMUNITY

Sin has hurt our ability to make and keep healthy relationships. Sometimes, instead of encouraging others to walk in God's ways, we settle for a weak kind of "acceptance" because we are afraid to speak hard truths. In other situations, we don't accept others until they've proven themselves to us. Our dysfunction in relationships is only healed when the Holy Spirit transforms our hearts through the gospel of grace. As we rely on God's Spirit, he enables us to give and receive grace in our relationships.

LESSON 5: A HUMBLE COMMUNITY

All of us want to be part of a community characterized not by self-centeredness but by selflessness and service. That humble kind of community brings glory to God and blesses humanity. But pride, which is another way of saying self-centeredness, gets in the way of that sort of community. To grow in humility, we need to identify pride in our lives and get rid of it by looking to Jesus as our example and experiencing his grace personally.

LESSON 6: HONEST RELATIONSHIPS

Authentic community requires honesty about ourselves and others. This is what the Bible calls walking in the light (1 John 1:7). The gospel assures us that God completely welcomes and approves of us in Christ.

But we struggle to apply this truth in our relationships. We hide behind a false self, and we shy away from speaking the truth to others. When we understand the gospel and have the Holy Spirit's help, we can walk in the light together, free to be known as we really are and to love others as they really are.

LESSON 7: A JOYFUL COMMUNITY

In this lesson, we'll look at another result of grasping the gospel of grace: joy. God is full of joy and sent Jesus so that his joy could be in us. God *justifies* and *sanctifies* everyone who trusts in Jesus; understanding justification and sanctification will help us to experience joy in Christ.

LESSON 8: A COMMUNITY ON A MISSION

Christian community always has an outward face, *moving toward others as God has moved toward us.* We are called to leave our comfortable spaces and social circles to move toward people who don't know Christ, becoming friends with them, loving them, and inviting them into the community of faith. The Father sent the Son, the Son sent the Spirit, and the Spirit sends everyone who believes in Jesus. As we are changed by the Holy Spirit through the gospel, we are a "sent" people, on mission together!

HOW TO USE THIS STUDY

The Gospel-Centered Community for Teens is designed for small group study. This is not a personal Bible study to work through on your own. It is meant to be engaged and discussed with a group.

Each lesson should take about an hour to complete. Our experience has shown that this content often creates deep and substantive conversation that can easily last longer than an hour. So plan accordingly, and be sure to honor the time commitment that your group has made.

There is no outside work required of participants. Likewise, it is not assumed that the group leader will be an expert theologian or long-standing Christian. The Leader's Guide walks you through each step of the discussion. Just relax and guide a good conversation.

Each lesson follows the same format, which includes these elements:

BIBLE CONVERSATION
We want to start by talking about the Bible together. Don't feel like you have to get too deep. We just want to start each discussion by pondering God's Word and preparing for the ideas that will be presented in the lesson.

ARTICLE
The written articles are the primary source of the teaching content for each lesson. Each week, your group will take a few minutes and read the article out loud together.

DISCUSSION
This section is where we communally process the concepts being taught in the article. Often the discussion will work in conjunction with the next section (the exercise) to help flesh out the teaching and apply it to our lives in concrete ways.

EXERCISE
Each exercise in this study is designed to help you make practical applications of the concepts being taught. Be sure to allow enough time for your group to adequately work through and discuss the exercises as directed. Some of the best conversation comes in the exercise!

WRAP-UP
The wrap-up gives the leader the chance to answer any last-minute questions, reinforce ideas, and, most importantly, spend some time praying as a group.

WHAT TO EXPECT

EXPECT TO BE CHALLENGED . . .

because most of us have reduced the gospel to something less than it is. As you work through each lesson, expect your thinking about the gospel to be challenged and expanded.

EXPECT THE HOLY SPIRIT . . .

to be the one ultimately responsible for the growth of your group, and for the change in each person's life—including your own. Relax and trust him.

EXPECT YOUR GROUP'S AGENDA TO INCLUDE . . .

an open, give-and-take discussion of the article, the questions, and the exercises.

EXPECT STRUGGLE . . .

and don't be surprised to find that your group is a mixture of enthusiasm, hope, and honesty, along with indifference, anxiety, skepticism, guilt, and covering up. We are all people who need Jesus every day.

EXPECT A GROUP LEADER . . .

who needs Jesus as much as you do. No leader should be put on a pedestal, so expect that your group leader will have the freedom to share openly about his or her own weaknesses, struggles, and sins.

LESSON

THE CHALLENGE OF COMMUNITY

BIG IDEA

We've all experienced loneliness. We've all felt left out, like we're looking at other people's relationships from the outside with our faces pressed against the window. We long for relationship. That's what people are wired for. But so often it's hard to find, and we're left feeling alone. On the flip side, when we do find relationships and are part of a community, they turn out to be hard—sometimes *really* hard, to the point where we just feel like giving up on other people. In this lesson, we'll take a quick look at the landscape of modern relationships. In the next lesson we'll see where our need for relationships came from, why they can be so painful, and what our source of hope is—because there *is* hope!

BIBLE CONVERSATION

There are two Bible readings for this lesson.

Read Psalm 142:1–5 aloud. This psalm is a prayer written by David, who later became King of Israel.

Then discuss these questions together:

- How is the writer of this psalm feeling?
- How would you describe his relationship with God?

Read 1 Corinthians 12:12–27 aloud. This passage feels very different from our first reading. Here, Paul gives us a picture of the church—the *community* of believers—as the body of Jesus.

Then discuss these questions together:

- Based on this description of the church as a body, what should the church be like?

- What stands out to you about this description? What do you especially like about it? What surprises you?

ARTICLE

THE CHALLENGE OF COMMUNITY

Imagine a sad, dull, rainy place.[1] Let's call it the "grey town." Small businesses line the streets, but they're all shabby now. Except for a line of people at a bus stop, the whole town looks deserted. There used to be folks living here, but they were always quarreling. Each person felt like all the others were inferior or snobby or inconvenient or just plain annoying. One by one, they got fed up with the other people and moved far away. As new inhabitants arrived, they too got fed up with the people around them, so they too moved far away—only they had to move even farther to get away from those who'd already moved far away. The population of this grey town eventually spread out over "astronomical distances"[2] so that everyone could live their own isolated little lives.

You might think this is the setting of a dystopian movie—and you wouldn't be far wrong. It's the vision of hell that C. S. Lewis gives in his book *The Great Divorce*.

Why does he depict hell this way? Because the selfishness of the inhabitants is so out of control that they're all cut off from one another. It's a picture of isolation, and living in isolation is miserable. It's not how humans are meant to live. We are created for relationship. We're meant to flourish—to experience joy and fullness—when we're in community.

WHAT IS COMMUNITY?

A community is a network of relationships—a group of people who are all connected to one another because they have something in common, like a hobby or a neighborhood or a church or a school or family ties. The youth group or class you're reading this with is a community, too.

Community is the spirit of togetherness and unity that a group can develop when relationships within it are strong.

This book focuses specifically on Christian community, where the main thing we have in common is that we belong to God and we love Jesus. In a healthy Christian community, people love, care for, enjoy, serve, and even challenge one another in good ways. Through your time in this book, we want you to experience this kind of healthy and health-giving community more and more.

WHAT KEEPS US FROM EXPERIENCING COMMUNITY?

C. S. Lewis's grey town is the opposite of community. We could call it an *anti*-community. His picture is extreme of course, but it shows us two different problems with real-world relationships.

On the one hand, isolation is sad and lonely (which is why Lewis used it in his vision of hell). And in today's world, many people—perhaps especially young people—feel disconnected. They may be very connected on social media, but they are disconnected from healthy, meaningful relationships.

On the other hand, being in relationship with other people can also be hard. Sometimes things are great of course; we feel connected, and we like to be with our friends or family. But other times we experience pain and frustration in these relationships. Or we can feel like we're not truly connecting at all—somehow our friends or family just don't *get* us.

It's easy to feel hopeless, like you can't live *with* people and you can't live *without* them.

The source of a lot of trouble in relationships is the self-focus that lives in our hearts and in the hearts of everyone around us. Focusing just on ourselves means we put our own desires, feelings, and plans ahead of other people and their desires, feelings, and plans. This self-focus—or selfishness—is evidence of what the Bible calls *sin*, and as we'll see in the next lesson, it is the result of rejecting God and his loving ways.

What does selfishness look like in ordinary life?

Maybe we bond with our friends by talking badly about other people. Maybe we insult someone directly, putting them down to lift ourselves up. Maybe we don't like the way a person is doing something, so we criticize them or try to take over. Maybe there are people on the margins that we don't have time for because we're too busy doing our own thing. Or maybe we're the ones on the margins, and we resent the people who seem to be ignoring us. Maybe we find some people boring or awkward, so we try to escape from conversations with them.

Often selfishness is buried inside us. When we feel bad about something we've done, we might look for someone or something we can blame so that we don't have to feel guilty. When we look at other people and think, *I can't measure up to them,* we might try to feel better by telling ourselves, *At least I don't do this* or, *At least I'm better at that.* Or we might hope other people mess up and secretly feel glad when they do.

These kinds of attitudes make it difficult to form and keep good relationships.

In a messed-up world in which we've all hurt others (sometimes intentionally, sometimes unintentionally), and we've all been hurt by others (sometimes intentionally, sometimes unintentionally), we instinctively develop ways of protecting ourselves. We become suspicious, imagining what other people might be thinking about us, or how they could hurt us if we got close. Here are some examples of how we try to protect ourselves:

- We act confident, stuffing our fears and hurt so far down we don't even realize they're there.
- We use humor as a shield so we don't feel pain.
- We become angry and confrontational.
- We construct a "safe" identity based on something we're good at (academics, sports, music, art, social causes, chess, etc.).

Whether they lead to dramatic blow ups or increasing distance in our relationships, our selfishness and self-protecting behaviors make relationships hard.

Selfishness and self-protection have been around for about as long as people have existed. Human nature hasn't changed since Adam and Eve's original fall into sin.

WHAT TECHNOLOGY ADDS TO THE MIX

What *has* changed? Technology. Texting. Social media. Group chats. Online gaming. These things offer unlimited entertainment and the appearance of community. Sharing photos, memes, music, videos, or little passing thoughts does create a certain kind of bond.

But this shiny technology has serious downsides.

One downside of life online is that it gives us new ways of seeing others succeed or fail, of gossiping, of hurting others, and of being hurt. And this can all happen more quickly and more publicly than ever before, heightening our embarrassment, anger, and insecurity when something goes wrong.

Another downside—and this will sound strange—is that technology makes everything too easy. It's easy to establish a surface connection—just like and follow! It's easy to *heart* something and never think about it again, and to count the hearts we get to feel validated. It's easy to create and curate the public identity we want, and for that identity to be threatened. It's easy to get a bunch of "sad face" reactions when we share something hard, and to *sad face* somebody else's hard thing and keep scrolling. It's easy to throw out insults and edgy memes. And it's easy to cut people off altogether: just unfollow and block them. Online connections can be a little too disposable.

This "too-easy-ness" is part of why screen-based relationships ultimately cannot meet our need for human connection.

In addition, technology makes it easy to create *many* online relationships—more relationships than we can possibly have the time or bandwidth to invest in and deepen.[3] Having lots and lots of shallow online relationships simply cannot feed our spirits in the same way that a few in-person, in-depth relationships can.

Here's an analogy. Trying to meet our need for relationship by picking up our phone is like trying to live on snack food from a vending machine. Eating a bunch of snacks will give you enough calories to stay alive, but your body won't run well, and eventually your inadequate diet will take its toll on your health. To be healthy, you need nutrients from real food.

Similarly, interactions on a screen can give us a weak connection with another person—or with many people—but they cannot fulfill our need for meaningful relationship. We must have real-life relationships to be emotionally healthy. In recent years, as virtual relationships have little by little taken the place of in-person relationships, we see greater levels of loneliness, anxiety, and depression in people who are starving for real human community.

BUT THERE'S HOPE!

Real-life, in-person relationships have a richness that digital relationships can never deliver. When someone tells you something in person, you can hear their tone of voice and read their body language. You can *really* laugh or cry together. You can *really* give someone a hug or a fist bump. You can have an in-depth discussion. You can play a game or do a service project or have lunch together.

When Jesus rescues us, he rescues us into a real community of flesh and blood people who have also been rescued. Now, in this community we will still face some of the emotional and relational challenges we looked at earlier. Relationships are still *hard*. But because of what God has done for us in Jesus and what he is still doing through the Holy Spirit, they are also *possible*. God is at work inside each individual and among all of us as a community so that we grow and flourish and reflect his grace to people around us.

What has God done? We'll read about that in the next lesson. Stay tuned!

DISCUSSION

Which statement or idea in this article stood out to you the most?

From what you've seen and experienced in your life, what makes relationships and community hard?

How do you see technology affecting your relationships?

In the article, you read that the group you're in now is a community, and that the goal of this book is to learn together how to grow into a community of people who love, care for, enjoy, serve, and even challenge one another. How does that make you feel? Excited? Nervous? Uncertain? Why do you think you feel that way?

EXERCISE

CONSIDERING MY CONNECTIONS

The goal of this exercise is to reflect on your relationships. You will start by making a list of friends and communities. Then you will explore how connected you feel. At the end, there are some questions to help you process your thoughts.

1. List significant relationships in your life. Consider both one-on-one relationships and communities/networks of relationships you are part of (close friends, family, teammates, church friends, organizations, youth group, etc.).

2. Look over the list you made, and then check the boxes that describe your overall feeling about the relationships you have.

☐ I feel well-connected. I am happy with the number of relationships I have and how deep they are.

☐ I feel somewhat connected, but I would like more relationships or more depth to the relationships I have.

☐ I don't feel very connected. I feel a need for more relationships in my life.

☐ I have people who encourage me in my relationship with God, but I would like to go deeper in these relationships.

☐ I don't really have people who encourage me in my relationship with God.

3. Think about this group specifically (the group with whom you're going through this book). Check the boxes that reflect your experience of this group.

☐ This group is well-connected. The members of the group are close, and I feel like I am part of this group.

☐ This group is somewhat connected. We get along, but we don't actually know each other that well.

☐ This group has smaller groups of people inside of it who are close to one another, but the group as a whole is not very well-connected.

☐ The people in this group do not seem well-connected to one another. It doesn't feel like I am part of a healthy community.

4. Based on the boxes you checked, take a few minutes to respond to these questions:

• What are you thankful for? What good, healthy things do you see in your relationships?

• What do want? Where would you like to see growth in your relationships?

- What do you need? What help do you need personally to pursue deeper community?

If you wish, share your answers with the group at the end of the exercise time.

Tip: You may wish to review your answers to these questions over the next several weeks. That will give you the opportunity to pray about your relationships and observe any growth or changes in them.

WRAP-UP

Ask any remaining questions, make final comments, and pray together that over the next several weeks, God would be working within each individual and within the group as a whole.

LESSON

THE BACKSTORY

BIG IDEA

We've talked about how community is something we all need. But where did that need come from? Is it just a matter of survival? No. As human beings we long for relationships that are meaningful—relationships in which we can know other people and be known by them. This longing comes from God himself. God is relational and loving. And he made humans in his image, meaning that we are like him in important ways. We can have meaningful relationships with him and with people around us. We can love others and be loved by them.

That sounds beautiful! But as we all know, relationships can be a source of pain and frustration. Why does this happen? What went wrong? In this lesson we'll explore why we have such a need for relationships, why they're so hard, and why we can have real hope in spite of the hard things. Then, as we continue through this book, we'll learn together—as a community—what healthy Christian community looks like.

BIBLE CONVERSATION

There are two Bible readings for this lesson.

Read Genesis 1:26–27, 31 aloud.

Then discuss these questions together:

- What are some things we learn about God in this passage?

- What are some things we learn about humanity in this passage?

Read Genesis 3:2–13 aloud.

Then discuss these questions together:

- What do you observe about the relationship between God and the humans he created? Consider their actions, words, and motivations.

- What do you observe about the relationship between Adam and Eve? Consider their actions, words, and motivations.

THE BACKSTORY

Superhero movies have been quite popular in recent years.

Now, it's certainly possible to watch a superhero movie without knowing how the hero got where they are. But as a viewer, you're more invested and you can follow events better if you know the character's backstory. That background information enables you to understand how the superhero got to be the way they are and what makes them tick. That's why all major superheroes have an origin story—and sometimes their sidekicks do, too.

In the last lesson, we saw that on the one hand, humans need community, yet on the other hand, connections with other people can be hard. Why are both these things true? A little background can help us understand how we got here.

WHERE DID THE IDEA OF COMMUNITY COME FROM?

People are different from one another, but we all have one thing in common: At some level, we all want community. We long to know others and be known by them. We treasure meaningful friendships that allow us to truly be ourselves. Though some of us haven't yet found this sort of community, and though some of us have been wounded by past relationships, all of us want and need authentic community.

Why? Our longing for connection is rooted in God himself. God is a relational being. He exists in community—Father, Son, and Spirit. It is a community defined by love (1 John 4:8). Out of his abundant, overflowing love and creativity and power, he made people in his image—people who could love and relate to him and to one another. In other words, God created us for community.

But if deep community is something we all want, why is it so rare? How come we have so much trouble experiencing the meaningful human relationships God wired us for? Why do we encounter all the problems we looked at in Lesson 1?

BROKEN COMMUNITY

The problem goes all the way back to the dawn of humanity.

The events of Genesis 3 and 4 are so long ago and far away that they may seem completely unrelatable at first. But when we look at them through the lens of relationship, we recognize some relationship issues.

You just read Genesis 1, in which God creates humans, and his evaluation of his creation is that "it was very good" (Genesis 1:31). Genesis 2 shows God taking good care of these humans and placing them in a garden paradise. It also shows how ecstatic Adam is when God introduces him to Eve. Adam instantly recognizes that they are just right for each other. The relationships between Adam and Eve and between them and God—a little community!—are perfectly loving and joyful.

But in Genesis 3 everything changes.

First, the relationship Adam and Eve have with God is broken. Adam and Eve question whether God is really truthful and wonder if he's been holding out on them. In the end, both of them betray their Creator and friend. As a consequence of their sin, Adam and Eve hide from God and are eventually forced to leave the garden. Their exile is a picture of how totally broken the relationship is between God and the two humans.

Second, the relationship between Adam and Eve is broken. In Genesis 2, they are naked and unashamed. In Genesis 3, they feel ashamed and try to cover their nakedness. Their rejoicing turns into hiding and blaming.

Things get even darker in Genesis 4. Adam and Eve's son Cain is jealous that God approves of Abel, and maybe also ashamed that he didn't give God his best, so he murders his brother Abel. When God asks him where Abel is, his response is defensive and self-protective: "Am I my brother's keeper?" (Genesis 4:9). He's basically saying, *Who cares about him? He's not my problem.*

THE MORE THINGS CHANGE, THE MORE THEY STAY THE SAME

Doubt. Mistrust. Lies about someone's character. Betrayal. Secrecy and hiding. Blame-shifting. Lashing out when you feel guilty. Jealousy. Hatred.

All these things have their beginnings in Genesis 3 and 4. Reading these chapters, we're able to see how all that selfishness is rooted in a rejection of God and his ways.

The results of sin were catastrophic, and Adam and Eve would never be able to put things back together on their own. They could not rescue themselves from sin and selfishness, and they could not escape God's judgment on their sin. Neither can we.

So God did the unthinkable. He sent his Son into the world. Jesus took on flesh and became one of us so that he could rescue us. Unlike Adam and Eve, he obeyed God fully. He lived a life of perfect love. Paul says that all who believe in Jesus are given his perfect record (Romans 4:5).

Then, by dying on the cross, Jesus took on the judgment that we humans deserved for our betrayal of God. He died so we could live, now and forever. In short, Jesus restores our relationship with God.

There is more. Jesus also restores our relationships with one another. John says that to those who receive Jesus, who believe in his name, he gives the right to be called children of God (John 1:12). In Christ, we are members of God's family.

God not only makes us part of his family, but he also gives us the Holy Spirit, who empowers us to love each other like family. As we live in relationship with God, his Spirit works in us. He causes us to grow, making us less and less self-centered, and more and more loving, like Jesus.

There's still hard stuff. Growth takes time. But we live in hope because we know we are all being changed. The Holy Spirit helps us do the hard work of community: forgiving one another, encouraging one another, bearing with one another, and "speaking the truth in love," which makes the body grow so that it "builds itself up in love" (Ephesians 4:15–16).

This is how we function in unity, as many diverse parts of one body.

In the next lesson, we'll begin delving into some of the ways the community of faith—the body of Christ—can be a blessing to everyone who's part of it.

DISCUSSION

Which statement or idea in this article stood out to you the most?

Why do human beings have a need for relationships?

How did Adam and Eve's disobedience affect our relationship with God? How did it affect our relationships with other people?

The article discusses many things God has done to overcome the effects of human selfishness and sin. Which of these things gives you special encouragement today?

THE SELF AND OTHERS

In our culture, we tend to view the individual—the self—as very important. We are encouraged to write our own story, which inevitably makes us the main character. We are encouraged to look within ourselves to discover who we are and to then express that to the world. Because the self is such a high value in our society, we can't always see how individualism can be harmful to relationships, or how it can cross the line into self-centeredness.

Directions:

- Under each heading below is a list of ways individualism or self-focus can express itself, depending on who you are and how you're wired. Read through each list.

- Check one item in each list that represents a tendency in your life.

- Answer the questions after each section based on the item that you checked.

- When you have worked your way through all of the lists, answer the final questions at the bottom.

- You'll have an opportunity to share at the end.

SELF-RELIANCE

☐ You want to deal with problems and challenges on your own, without help from others.

☐ It's hard for you to be vulnerable about what's really going on with you because you think, "Those are my issues to deal with."

☐ You don't really believe that you need people to grow spiritually; you can do just fine on your own with Bible study, prayer, and Christian videos or articles online.

☐ It's hard for you to receive gifts or help from people without wanting to pay them back somehow.

Questions for the item you checked:

- How do you think this way of thinking gets in the way of healthy community?

- How would the opposite way of thinking contribute to healthy community?

SELF-PROTECTION

☐ You want to be thought of as a "good Christian" by others, and hardly anybody knows you as you really are.

☐ Your relationships stay on the surface. You may share *some* things with other people, but only what you want them to know. You do not want them to dig deeper.

☐ When relationships get hard, you tend to pull away rather than deal with the issues.

☐ You tend to keep others at arm's length to guard yourself from being hurt or rejected.

☐ You fear at times that if people knew "the real you," they wouldn't like you.

☐ You avoid conflict. If people offend you or hurt your feelings, you prefer to say nothing rather than risk having them get angry at you or reject you.

☐ Your sense of self-worth rises and falls depending on what other people think of you.

Questions for the item you checked:

- How do you think this way of thinking gets in the way of healthy community?

- How would the opposite way of thinking contribute to healthy community?

SELF-IMPORTANCE AND SELF-WILL

☐ You try to stay busy all the time; it's the way you fill the hole in your life because close relationships just aren't there.

☐ You care about what others think of your abilities and accomplishments *more* than you care about what they think of you as a friend (kind, generous, etc.).

☐ You regularly choose schoolwork, extracurriculars, or hobbies over people.

☐ Your schedule and priorities always take precedence; you don't reshuffle your agenda to help or serve others.

☐ You like having people around, but you don't tend to take their advice.

Questions for the item you checked:

- How do you think this way of thinking gets in the way of healthy community?

- How would the opposite way of thinking contribute to healthy community?

Final questions:

- Take a minute to ask God what he wants to say to you about community. Write down what comes to mind.

- What is your main takeaway from this lesson?

SHARE

Take a few minutes to allow members of the group to volunteer to share what they discovered in doing this exercise.

WRAP-UP

Ask any remaining questions, make final comments, and pray together that over the next several weeks God would be working within each individual and within the group as a whole.

3

HOW DO WE DO CHRISTIAN COMMUNITY?

BIG IDEA

In the last lesson we learned that we need community because God made us in his image to be in relationship with him and one another. We looked at how self-centeredness can make community hard, and we traced the relational problems people have back to their original decision to reject God and his ways. Finally, we turned to the good news: Through the life, death, and resurrection of Jesus we can be delivered from our selfishness and set free to love one another through the power of the Holy Spirit. That leaves a practical but important question: What *is* Christian community, and how does it work? We'll see that an essential quality of Christian community is *faith expressing itself through love*. This means that faith in all God has given us through Jesus is what moves and enables us to love others. Let's investigate how that works.

BIBLE CONVERSATION

There are two Bible readings for this lesson.

Read Luke 6:32–36 aloud.

Then discuss these questions together:

- According to Jesus, how do people generally tend to interact with one another?

- In contrast, how does Jesus call his followers to interact with other people?

Read Acts 2:42–45 aloud. This passage describes what community looked like among the very early Christians.

Then discuss these questions together:

- What do you like about the community that's described in this passage?

- What do you think made it possible for these believers to have this kind of community?

HOW DO WE DO CHRISTIAN COMMUNITY?

You scratch my back, and I'll scratch yours. One hand washes the other. Quid pro quo. Tit for tat. The idea behind all these expressions is this: "I'll do something for you if you do something for me"—or, in the case of tit for tat, "I'll do something *to* you if you do something to me." Why do we have so many phrases to express this idea? The answer to that question tells us something about human nature.

A PRINCIPLE OF HUMAN NATURE

We've developed multiple expressions for *I do something for you, you do something for me* because it's such a common way of relating to others. It just makes sense to us. So if I help you, I expect you to help me in return. If you give me something, I feel like I owe you. And if you do something bad to me, I feel justified in doing something bad to you.

We bring this way of thinking into our communities, too. We look at our connections with others in terms of what they do for *us*—and we want to get at least as much out of them as we put into them. We expect our friends to give our lives meaning, keep us from being lonely, support us in hard times, celebrate with us in good times, and help us accomplish our goals. But thinking about relationships in a self-focused way keeps us from experiencing the fullness of what God meant for them to be.

A DIFFERENT WAY

Instead of putting ourselves at the center of our relationships, instead of seeing our relationships as being about ourselves and our feelings, God wants us to see *him* at the center of our relationships. He plans to use our relationships to change us and help us grow spiritually. And he plans to use them to bless our friends, too. Let's contrast the two ways of viewing relationships.

When I am at the center:	When God is at the center:
What do I get from this? (How does this serve me?)	What can I give to this? (How can I serve?)
I define who I am, and then express that to others. Community is just an audience that affirms and validates me and my life.	God defines who we are, and we are secure in his love. From that place of security, we speak truth in love to one another.
Every *conflict* leads to polarization: me vs. you. If we can't agree, then we simply move on.	It's not me *vs.* you because we are not the authority. God is. So now it's me *and* you, seeking God together.
I think *economically* about relationships: I talk about anything I don't want to do in terms of what it costs me, the "expense" of time and energy. I may still do it because it's the "right thing to do," but I will *grumble*.	I am learning to think *graciously* about relationships. Things I don't want to do in my flesh become an opportunity to rely on the Spirit, and grumbling gets replaced by *gratitude*.
The focus of the community is inward—it is all about us. We don't look beyond our own needs.	Community has an outward face. The purpose of the community in Genesis 2 is to fill the earth. Jesus commissioned us to make disciples of all nations. We meet each other's needs, of course, but we are always moving toward others and inviting them in.

The Bible shows us what God-centered relationships are like. We see Jesus, filled with love and compassion, selflessly reaching out to other people again and again, meeting them in their place of need.

The Bible also tells Christians,

- "Love one another with brotherly affection. Outdo one another in showing honor" (Romans 12:10 ESV*).*

- "Be kind and compassionate to one another, forgiving each other, just as in Christ God forgave you" (Ephesians 4:32).

- "Everyone should be quick to listen, slow to speak and slow to become angry" (James 1:19).

- "Serve one another humbly in love" (Galatians 5:13).

- "Comfort one another, agree with one another, live in peace" (2 Corinthians 13:11).

None of this is easy! What's the secret sauce that makes such relationships possible?

HOW IT WORKS

When we read how Jesus related to others and how Christians are commanded to treat one another, we probably think, "That looks like a great way to live." But we might also recognize that all too often, our lives don't look like that.

When we see a gap between the Bible and our lives, we're tempted to respond in one of two ways. One way is to tell ourselves that we need to get our act together and try harder to be a nice person. This leads to hypocrisy, judgment of others, stress, and burnout. The other way is to say, "Yeah, there's no way I'm ever going to live up to that standard," and just give up. This leads to a stagnant life with little to no growth.

Neither of these responses will bring about healthy lives and community.

Paul wrote the book of Galatians to Christians who were divided over the issue of whether believers still needed to obey the Old Testament laws—especially the law saying that men had to be circumcised. Paul spends four chapters explaining that they do *not* still need to obey these laws. He sums up his point in this verse: "For *in Christ Jesus* neither circumcision nor uncircumcision has any value. The only thing that counts is *faith expressing itself through love*" (Galatians 5:6, emphasis added).

In Christ Jesus. That's the gospel. We are united with Jesus through faith. Being in Christ means he has taken away the punishment for our sin and given us credit for his perfect life. It means that because of his death and resurrection, we have new life. We have a new identity as someone who is "in Christ Jesus."

When this gospel truth really sinks in, it changes everything about how we live. We can stop worrying about whether we're doing enough to please God, make other people happy, or see ourselves as a "good person." Circumcision didn't have any value for the Galatians, and neither do any of the things we do to try to earn approval from God, other people, or ourselves. We're safe because we belong to God. Our identity is secure in Jesus. We can be at peace.

With all that worry off our shoulders, we're free to look around to see who we can love. Because what matters now—and what empowers our new life in community—is faith expressing itself through love.

It's not faith by itself. It's not love by itself. It's *faith expressing itself through love.* This means two things:

- Faith leads to real love, and faith is the energy that powers love.

- If there's no love, it means there's no real faith. An absence of love is a clear sign that faith is also absent.

What does this mean for community?

- When we have failed to love someone (in general or at a particular moment), it's a faith issue. We've taken our eyes off God and put ourselves back in the center of the relationship. We've forgotten that our identity is in God; we are his much-loved children, and he gives us whatever we need.

- Our faith enables us to admit it when haven't loved someone. We don't have to be ashamed or afraid—we have taken the gospel to heart! In Jesus, we're forgiven, and we can feel peace because of God's love for us. Being secure in Jesus means we can also be humble enough to ask the person for forgiveness for what we did.

So when we see a lack of love in our lives, we should look for our lack of faith—where are we not living in light of the gospel? And when we struggle to love others, we should ask God to give us more faith to trust him. We will grow in love for others as we absorb the love God has for us, lean on the perfect record Jesus has earned for us, and rely on the power the Holy Spirit gives us. Our faith expresses itself in love.

This simple truth is what gospel-centered community is built on. The way to build deeper community (*love*) is to delight in the gospel more fully (*faith*). As we embrace everything we have received in Jesus and invite the Holy Spirit to work it into our hearts and lives, we'll start to love others. When we mess up, we'll admit it, receive God's grace and forgiveness, and continue to move toward others as God has moved toward us.

DISCUSSION

What stood out to you in the article? Anything new, interesting, or challenging?

How is the way God has treated us different from the "You do something for me, I'll do something for you" way of interacting?

Look at the chart that contrasts relationships with self at the center and relationships with God at the center (p. 32). Which have you experienced? How do you feel about your experience?

EXERCISE

FAITH EXPRESSING ITSELF THROUGH LOVE

"The only thing that counts is
faith expressing itself through love." (Galatians 5:6)

The goal of this exercise is to apply "faith expressing itself through love" to our everyday lives. There are two parts; each has a group discussion, individual reflection, and then group sharing.

PART 1: Why is it hard for us to love others?

Group Discussion: Read these specific ways the Bible commands us to love one another. Circle the one that you find most challenging.

- "Do not let any unwholesome talk come out of your mouths, but only what is helpful for building others up according to their needs" (Ephesians 4:29).

- "Everyone should be quick to listen, slow to speak and slow to become angry" (James 1:19).

- "Warn those who are lazy. Encourage those who are timid. Take tender care of those who are weak. Be patient with everyone" (1 Thessalonians 5:14 NLT).

- "Accept one another, then, just as Christ accepted you, in order to bring praise to God" (Romans 15:7).

- "Be kind and compassionate to one another, forgiving each other, just as in Christ God forgave you" (Ephesians 4:32).

- "Serve one another humbly in love" (Galatians 5:13).

Briefly share with each other which one you chose, and then move on to the individual reflection.

Individual Reflection:

a. Why did you choose this answer?

b. Why do you find it hard to do this?

c. Think of a time when you really didn't *want* to obey this command, or you felt like you just *couldn't*.

d. When you were in that situation, what do you remember thinking . . .

   . . . about God?

   . . . about yourself?

   . . . about the other person or people you are called to love?

Group Sharing: Share what you learned about yourself (how you relate to people) from this reflection. Then move on to Part 2 together.

PART 2: How does the gospel help us love others?

Group Discussion: The article discussed a better way of living: "faith expressing itself through love." This means deeply knowing and relying on the gospel of God's love so that we are free to love others without being wrapped up in ourselves.

Let's look again at the many things God has given everyone who believes in him. What else could we add to this list?

- his love

- status as his child

- the record for Jesus's perfect life

- forgiveness—all our sins are erased

- rescue so that we don't have to endure his punishment

- the new life we receive from Jesus's death and resurrection

- the Holy Spirit, who lives and works inside us

- _____

- _____

- _____

Individual Reflection:

a. Think again about the situation you chose in the first section: Which of these gospel truths seems most relevant to that situation?

b. If you had believed that truth in the moment, how might it have changed the way you thought about God, yourself, and the other person?

c. How might those thoughts have changed your behavior?

Group Sharing: Discuss your answers together.

WRAP-UP

Ask any remaining questions, make final comments, and pray together that with the help of the Holy Spirit, everyone in the group would grow in understanding "faith expressing itself through love" and see it in their lives more and more.

A GRACE-FILLED COMMUNITY

BIG IDEA

Because we are made in the image of God, we all long to be part of an accepting, loving community. But sin has hurt our ability to make and keep healthy relationships. Sometimes, instead of encouraging others to walk in God's ways, we settle for a weak kind of "acceptance" because we are afraid to speak hard truths to them. In other situations, we don't accept others until they've proven themselves to us. Our dysfunction in relationships is only healed when the Holy Spirit transforms our hearts and lives through the gospel of grace. *Grace* refers to all God's blessings of love and salvation—blessings that we don't deserve and could never earn. When we believe deep down that God graciously accepts and forgives us in Christ, we understand what it means to accept and forgive one another. As we rely on God's Spirit, he enables us to give and receive grace in our relationships. This is how we become a grace-filled community.

BIBLE CONVERSATION

We will read two passages this week. As you read, look for what each passage says or shows about grace. Remember that grace means love and blessings that we don't deserve.

Read Luke 7:36–47 aloud.

Then discuss these questions together:

- Why does the Pharisee reject the woman's actions?

- Why does Jesus accept the woman's actions?

- What is the difference between the woman and the Pharisee?

Read Titus 3:3–8 aloud.

Then discuss these questions together:

- What words in this passage describe what our gracious God has done for us?

- How does God's grace change us? What does it enable us to do?

A GRACE-FILLED COMMUNITY

The gospel is at the heart of Christian community. And at the heart of the gospel is God's grace. When we talk about grace, we mean God's love and goodness toward us that we don't deserve and could never earn: "God shows his love for us in that while we were still sinners, Christ died for us" (Romans 5:8 ESV). The grace of God saves us, blesses us, and keeps us secure. But how does grace shape a community?

To answer that question, let's consider two things that work against grace in our hearts: **pride** and **fear**.

PRIDE AND FEAR

When we're filled with **pride**, we do not want to admit we have a problem. We don't want to face the fact that we've sinned and we can't fix it. We want to prove ourselves so that God will accept us. Have you ever told God that you would "never do that again"? Or thought that if you could just get a fresh start, you would do better? When we say things like this, we may think we're asking for grace, but what we really want is a second chance to *earn* God's favor instead of receiving it freely. We want to justify ourselves before God—prove that we're right—but the Bible is clear: We have been "justified by his grace" (Titus 3:7 ESV).

Then there's **fear**. Our fear makes us think that God does not accept us. We think that God cannot forgive what we've done, or at least that he is tired of dealing with the same thing over and over. So instead of asking for forgiveness, we try to hide our sin because we fear his rejection. But the good news is that because of Jesus we can "approach God's throne of grace with confidence, so that we may receive mercy and find grace to help us in our time of need" (Hebrews 4:16).

When there's pride or fear in our relationship with God, it shows up in our relationships with people, too. Pride and fear get in the way of genuine community.

Pride makes us want to look good so people will accept us. We can feel this pressure in any group. We are driven by whatever we think will get the approval of the people around us, even at church. Not only that, we also grade other people based on how well they live up to those standards. Pride can make us insecure and judgmental all at once!

Our **fear** leads us to try to protect ourselves. We're afraid people wouldn't like us if they really knew us. We don't want to be judged or rejected, so we excuse our sin, blame it on others, hide it, lie about it—anything but admit it. Think about this: How often do people in your community admit they've sinned against someone and ask for forgiveness? We usually avoid this because we're afraid of being known as we really are. But hiding our sin stifles true community.

Pride and fear are like two sides of the same coin—both are rooted in self-concern. Consider a few ways that our self-concern hinders community:

- We avoid people who don't fit in with what our community thinks is popular or acceptable.
- We make our conversations about us and our strengths.
- We don't share in group settings unless we know the "right" things to say.
- We are slow to accept new people to our community until they prove themselves as trustworthy.
- We only share struggles that seem acceptable.

Pride and fear often keep us from sharing what is really going on in our lives. But when someone in a group lets go of fear and embraces honesty, they usually find that people do not shun or shame them. Instead, they move toward them with grace and support. Then others feel encouraged to be honest too. This is how grace brings a community closer together.

THE WORK OF THE HOLY SPIRIT

Letting go of pride and fear to become a caring, grace-filled community isn't easy! We need the help of the Holy Spirit, who reminds us of the grace God has given us in Christ. First Peter 3:18 sums up the gospel this way: "Christ suffered for our sins once for all time. He never sinned, but he died for sinners to bring you safely home to God. He suffered physical death, but he was raised to life in the Spirit" (NLT). When we receive the grace of God in Christ, our fear and pride are put to death, and we are brought to life spiritually by God's Holy Spirit.

As the Holy Spirit works grace into our hearts, the assurance of God's love drives out our pride and fear. Let's look at some changes that occur as the Holy Spirit fills us with grace:

- In our *pride*, we are biased toward those we like or those who can help us, but Jesus welcomed the outcasts. Now, by his Spirit we "show no partiality" (James 2:1 ESV).

- In our *pride*, we are envious when good things happen to others, but Jesus put our good before his own. Now, by his Spirit we "rejoice with those who rejoice, [and] weep with those who weep" (Romans 12:15 ESV).

- In our *pride,* we hold grudges and are unwilling to forgive, but Jesus forgave both his enemies who crucified him and his friends who deserted him. Now, by his Spirit we "bear with each other and forgive one another" (Colossians 3:13).

- In our *fear*, we try to control people and situations, but Jesus surrendered control and went willingly to the cross. Now, by his Spirit we can walk in "humility and gentleness" (Ephesians 4:2 ESV).

- In our *fear*, we want to run when relationships get difficult, but Jesus endured the cross for those who sinned against him. Now, by his Spirit we can "be patient, bearing with one another in love" (Ephesians 4:2).

- In our *fear*, we are afraid to confront the sins of others, but Jesus dealt honestly with sin. Now, by his Spirit, when someone is struggling with sin, we can "gently and humbly help that person back onto the right path" (Galatians 6:1 NLT).

We won't do this perfectly. This is why forgiveness is essential, and it is God's grace that enables us to forgive others as he has forgiven us.

As the Holy Spirit works in the people in our group—helping us deal with our pride and fear, and helping us love one another as God has loved us—we will grow together into a gospel-centered, grace-filled community.

DISCUSSION

Have you ever been in a community where you felt accepted (not perfectly, of course, but genuinely)? What made you feel that way?

Did you feel like you could relate to any of the examples of pride or fear in the article? Explain.

On a scale from 1 to 10 (1 being low, 10 being high), how grace-filled would you say our community is? Why did you choose the number you did?

GROWING IN GRACE

One of the greatest blessings of the gospel is the presence and power of the Holy Spirit, who lives in every one of God's people (Romans 8:9–11). To grow in grace means to continually rely on the Spirit's power rather than on our own instincts or preferences.

This exercise is designed to help us reflect more deeply on how the Holy Spirit can change us.

The chart on the next page shows six ways that our pride and fear get in the way of community.

Directions:

Read each row from left to right. As you read . . .

- Check the sinful tendencies on the left that sometimes keep you from accepting other people.
- Check the aspects of the Holy Spirit's work (on the right) that you find the most appealing or that you would most like to see in yourself.

SIX SPECIFIC WAYS THAT OUR PRIDE AND FEAR HINDER COMMUNITY:

These Sinful (Non-Accepting) Tendencies →	Are Rooted in Pride or Fear	But Now →	The Holy Spirit Makes It Possible for Us to Love and Accept One Another.
☐ **Favoritism:** I sometimes show preference toward those I like or those who can help me.	These people have earned my respect, or these people have something I need. They are more desirable than others who have less to offer.	But now →	☐ "Believers . . . must not show favoritism" (James 2:1). The Spirit helps me to treat every person with love, patience, and kindness, honoring them as image-bearers of God.
☐ **Control:** I sometimes use my relational ability to manipulate people or situations.	I am trying to manipulate people to do what I think is "right." If they do what I want, I am more accepting of them.	But now →	☐ "Be completely humble and gentle" (Ephesians 4:2). The Spirit moves me to humility (my rules are not the standard), which frees me to love others whether or not they "play by my rules."
☐ **Avoidance:** I sometimes escape or avoid people when relationships get difficult.	These people are not living up to what I expect of them, so they're not worthy of my acceptance. I guess that's "just the way these people are" (but if they want to be that way, then I don't want to relate to them).	But now →	☐ "Be patient, bearing with one another in love" (Ephesians 4:2). The Spirit gives me patience to bear with others, love to believe the best about them, and faithfulness to stay engaged with them, even with all their faults and failures. The Spirit gives me the strength to move toward them as God moved toward me.

☐ **Peacekeeping:** I hesitate to speak to others about sinful patterns in their lives, even when I'm close to them.	Everyone has faults and weaknesses. Who am I to judge someone else? Live and let live.	But now →	☐ "Restore [others] in a spirit of gentleness" (Galatians 6:1 ESV). The Spirit gives me a true love for others, which means that I want to see them glorify God fully. I am sad about their sin (not just annoyed with it) and motivated by love to speak to them gently and with humility, knowing that I am also a sinner saved by grace.
☐ **Party Spirit or Cliquishness:** I just relate better to "these people" rather than "those people," so that's who I hang out with.	These people are more like me, so I accept and defend what they believe, say, or do. After all, what they believe, say, or do is "right"! But *those people* are different. The things they believe, say, or do are terrible.	But now →	☐ Have "no divisions among you" (1 Corinthians 1:10 ESV). The Spirit brings unity and peace within the body of Christ, causing me to love *everyone*, even those who are not like me. The Spirit triumphs over all divisions, whether based on class/social status, race/ethnicity, politics, family, ways of thinking or dressing, taste, or anything else that can divide people.
☐ **Unforgiving Spirit:** I struggle to forgive this person or these people; their offenses against me are too willful, too consistent, or too hurtful.	I'm not as bad or hurtful as they are; their sin against me is much worse than my sin against God and others. If I forgave them, they'd essentially "get away with it." Where would the justice be then?	But now →	☐ "Bear with each other and forgive one another if any of you has a grievance against someone. Forgive as the Lord forgave you" (Colossians 3:13). The Spirit enables me to be gracious and forgiving toward the faults and failures of others. I can trust God to bring redemption and justice.

When everyone is finished, take a few minutes to allow members of the group to volunteer to share what they found in doing this exercise.

WRAP-UP

Ask any remaining questions and make final comments. Then pray together that the Holy Spirit would help everyone in the group feel loved and secure in the grace God has given them and that he would help them extend grace to others.

5

A HUMBLE COMMUNITY

BIG IDEA

One feature of a gospel-centered community is humility. All of us want to be part of a community where self-centeredness is dead, and selflessness and service are alive and well. That kind of community brings glory to God and blesses humanity. So what gets in the way of that sort of community? Pride, which is another way of saying self-centeredness. We've seen that pride gets in the way of receiving grace from God and giving it to others. Pride also keeps us from being humble. To grow in humility, we need to identify the ways pride shows up in our lives, and we need to get rid of pride by looking to Jesus as our example and experiencing his grace personally. The aim of this lesson is to help you understand humility, grow into a humbler person, and become part of a humbler community that is eager to serve.

BIBLE CONVERSATION

We are going to read a conversation between Jesus and two of his disciples about true greatness. As we read, pay attention to the different characters in the story and what we can learn from each one.

Read Mark 10:35–45 aloud.

Then discuss these questions together:

- In plain language, what do James and John want?
- Why do the other disciples respond the way they do?
- What does Jesus say about himself (the Son of Man)?
- What point is Jesus making about the kingdom of God?

HUMILITY AND COMMUNITY

Mother Teresa was a nun who spent her life serving the poor in the slums of Kolkata, India. She described her mission as serving "the hungry, the naked, the homeless, the crippled, the blind, the lepers, all those people who feel unwanted, unloved, uncared for throughout society, people that have become a burden to the society and are shunned by everyone."[4]

Mother Teresa never sought fame or power—yet she ended up with both. She won the Nobel Peace Prize. She inspired millions. She influenced presidents and kings. She died in 1997, but she is one of the most admired humanitarians in recent history.

All of us feel a desire to honor a person like Mother Teresa. Why? Because she considered other people's needs above her own.

HUMBLE SERVANT OR PRIDEFUL CONSUMER?

All of us wish we could be part of a community where people truly look out for one another and do what they can to meet others' needs—a community where self-centeredness is left behind, and generous service is embraced. This is the kind of community the Bible urges us toward: "Don't be selfish; don't try to impress others. Be *humble*, thinking of others as better than yourselves. Don't look

THE GOSPEL-CENTERED COMMUNITY FOR TEENS

out only for your own interests, but take an interest in others, too" (Philippians 2:3–4 NLT, emphasis added).

Notice that the key to serving others is **humility**. If we want to be a community that serves others in love, then we need to pursue humility.

What does it mean to be humble? It means seeing yourself as you really are: I sin and make mistakes. I'm no better than anyone else. I really needed Jesus to rescue me. I'm loved dearly by God, but I'm definitely not the center of the universe.

We can embrace these truths about ourselves because we remember the grace we have received. Humility says, "God has given me his love and security and everything else I need. I don't need to stand on my rights and get everything I think I deserve." Humility gives us the attitude of a **servant**, someone who loves God and helps other people. It makes healthy, loving community possible.

The opposite of humility is pride. Pride says, "People owe me. I deserve _____. I should be getting something out of my relationships." Pride turns us into a **consumer**, someone who thinks mostly about what they want and what they can get from others.

The table below contrasts the ways a consumer and a servant look at community:

Pride: A Consumer . . .	Humility: A Servant . . .
Asks, "What's in it for me?"	Asks, "How can I serve others?"
Asks, "Who's going to relate to me and meet my needs?"	Asks, "Who can I relate to and whose needs can I meet?"
Is critical of the community's faults and weaknesses	Looks for God's grace at work in the community
Chooses to interact with people who make them feel good or who can do something for them	Appreciates the God-given gifts that everyone in the community has
Uses others	Empowers others for the good of God's family

The heart of pride is *self-concern*. Prideful self-concern can look different in different people. In some, it looks like arrogance and boasting. In others, it looks like self-protection and fear of people. But either way, it's pride and it kills community. We've all been in a community where everyone seems to enjoy each other, but below the surface each person is focused on themselves: worried about what others think of them, anxious about their needs, desperate for attention, insecure or self-righteous as they compare themselves with others, and so on. No matter what our self-concern looks like, it keeps us from loving others. When we're filled with pride and selfishness, we become consumers "shopping" for relationships that benefit us, not servants trying to care for others.

There can also be self-concern on a group level, and it looks like this: We're getting what we want from our own little community, so we don't welcome new people into our group, and we don't really care about the needs of the people outside it. We might even judge them and feel like we're better than they are.

Being a self-absorbed consumer shows a lack of faith. We worry about what others think because we don't understand how much God loves and even delights in us (Psalm 149:4), or because we think God's love and delight aren't *enough* for us. We are anxious because we don't believe God will meet our needs (Matthew 6:32). We try to make sure other people know about the good things we do because it's not enough for us that God sees and rewards us (Matthew 6:6). We compare ourselves to others because we forget that the only righteousness, the only goodness, we have comes from Jesus (1 Corinthians 1:30). Consumers are self-focused; they are all about building their own little kingdoms in order to meet their own needs and fulfill their own desires. But Jesus calls us to the opposite: "Seek first his kingdom and his righteousness, and all these things will be given to you as well" (Matthew 6:33).

GRACE FREES US TO SERVE

If you trust God to meet your needs, you are free from all that self-centered worry and striving, which means you are free to consider the needs of others. When that happens, you begin to understand this paradox: As long as I'm focused on getting my needs met, I will never get my needs met. But when I begin to meet the needs of others—living for them instead of for myself—I find that God graciously takes care of my needs in the process.

God's grace turns us into servants. Instead of demanding that others serve us, we joyfully let go of our rights and seek to serve God and others. It all begins with humility, which we only get by depending on Jesus and understanding deep down what the gospel means for our lives.

Jesus is the One who shows us perfectly what it means to be a humble servant. Paul sums up Jesus's humble life in Philippians 2. After he tells us to consider others more important than ourselves, he says,

> In your relationships with one another, have the same
> mindset as Christ Jesus:
>> Who, being in very nature God,
>>> did not consider equality with God something to be
>> used to his own advantage;
>> rather, he made himself nothing
>>> by taking the very nature of a servant,
>>> being made in human likeness. (Philippians 2:5–7)

Jesus had a right to be served simply because he is God, but instead of clinging to that right, Jesus became human—not a wealthy, influential human, but a humble servant: "The Son of Man did not come to be served, but to serve, and to give his life as a ransom for many" (Mark 10:45).

Jesus humbly served others throughout his ministry. He taught his disciples, healed sick people, and welcomed those his society looked down on—women, children, people with leprosy, people of different ethnicities—relying at every step on his heavenly Father through prayer. Ultimately, "he humbled himself in obedience to God and died a criminal's death on a cross" (Philippians 2:8 NLT).

We know that's not the end of the story. God raised his faithful servant from the dead and "elevated him to the place of highest honor" (Philippians 2:9 NLT). And from heaven, Jesus still serves us personally so that we can experience his grace.

Knowing that this grace is something we could never earn humbles us. This is how Paul could say, "Christ Jesus came into the world to save sinners—of whom I am the worst. But for that very reason I was shown mercy so that in me, the worst of sinners, Christ Jesus might display his immense patience as an example for those who would believe in him and receive eternal life" (1 Timothy 1:15–16).

Through the gospel, the Holy Spirit transforms our hearts to change us from selfish consumers to faithful servants of Christ. As servants of Christ, we live to serve others, for Jesus's sake and for God's glory: "For what we preach is not ourselves, but Jesus Christ as Lord, and ourselves as your servants for Jesus' sake" (2 Corinthians 4:5). As this penetrates our hearts, we will be eager to bless not just each other, but the world around us as well.

God's grace toward us in Christ needs to get deep down into our hearts in order to change us. We need to admit the ways we resist grace and resist being served by Jesus. We have to "give up" and allow him to serve us because we desperately need him to. And we need to reflect on the gracious humility he has shown us so that our hearts are softened and changed. Then we will find ourselves growing in joy and selflessness as we delight in serving him by serving others.

DISCUSSION

1. What idea stood out to you most in this article?

2. Look at the chart in the article.

   - On the consumer side, which attitudes or actions do you identify with personally? What negative effects do you think this has on your relationships or your involvement in community?

   - On the servant side, which attitudes or actions do you identify with personally (either something that you are growing in now or an area where you want to grow)? Would you say that you see this kind of humility and servanthood in your community?

   - For many people, serving God is really a way to pay him back or get him to owe them something. Have you ever found yourself doing that? What would it look like for you or for the group to be motivated by grace instead?

EXERCISE

PRIDE AND PREJUDICE

As we have seen, **pride** is about **self-concern**. The list below lists some patterns of self-concern. Check the ones you can see in yourself.

PART 1: The Individual

- ☐ I usually want to be in control.
- ☐ I see most issues as black and white and tend to view people as either for me or against me.
- ☐ I feel threatened by people who have different opinions. I avoid disagreements.
- ☐ I am often insensitive; I don't take other people's feelings into account.
- ☐ I tend to be closed-minded and committed to my own way of seeing things.
- ☐ I see other gifted, competent people as competition.
- ☐ I can be very critical of others.
- ☐ I have a hard time seeing or admitting my sins, mistakes, and faults.
- ☐ I like to do things myself; I have a hard time letting other people do things because I'm afraid they'll do them wrong.
- ☐ I really want everyone to respect me.

- ☐ I usually avoid leadership; I'm afraid to take charge.
- ☐ I see most issues as shades of gray. I'm reluctant to stand up for anything.
- ☐ I feel paralyzed by people who disagree with me. I spend lots of time and energy thinking about disagreements or responding to them in my head.
- ☐ I defer a lot to the feelings of others; I don't want to hurt anyone's feelings.
- ☐ I welcome new ideas and viewpoints too easily. I don't have many strong convictions or opinions.
- ☐ I rarely disagree with others, even when something is really wrong.
- ☐ I am often paralyzed because I'm so aware of my sins, mistakes, and faults.
- ☐ I want everybody to have a voice in every decision.
- ☐ I want to be liked by everyone.

Now choose one of the patterns you checked and think about the questions below. (If you have time, you may consider the questions for other patterns you checked.)

- How does this pattern reveal self-concern?

- How does this pattern hold you back from glorifying God and serving others?

- How might worshipping Jesus more deeply for what he has done help to free you from this pattern of self-concern?

PART 2: The Group

Think together about your group as a whole. Discuss the following questions:

- In what ways does our group display a consumer mindset rather than a servant mindset?

- What would it take for our group to move from being consumers in these areas to being humble servants, to each other and to people outside the group?

WRAP-UP

Ask any remaining questions, make final comments, and pray together, asking the Holy Spirit to help everyone in the group gain freedom from prideful self-concern and grow in humility and service to others.

6

HONEST RELATIONSHIPS

BIG IDEA

Real, authentic community requires being honest about ourselves and others. This is what the Bible calls walking in the light (1 John 1:7; Ephesians 5:8–9). The gospel assures us that, in spite of our sins and weakness, God completely welcomes and approves of us in Christ. But we struggle to apply this truth in our relationships. We hide behind a false self, putting our best foot forward. And we shy away from speaking the truth to others. When we understand the gospel and have the Holy Spirit's help, we can strengthen one another as we walk in the light together, free to be known as we really are and to love others as they really are.

BIBLE CONVERSATION

Today we are going to do two readings.

The first reading is a section of a letter by John, one of Jesus's disciples. In these verses, John makes a contrast between light (and the things that go with light) and darkness (and the things that go with darkness).

Read 1 John 1:5–9 aloud.

Then discuss these questions together:

- Explore John's contrast between light and darkness by filling in this chart:

What kinds of ideas are connected to light?	What kinds of ideas are connected to darkness?

- Based on the things you listed, what do you think it looks like for us to "walk in the light"?

The second reading is from Paul's letter to the believers in Ephesus. Read Ephesians 4:15, 25–32 aloud.

Then discuss the following question together:

- Based on this passage, how should Christians speak with one another?

HONEST RELATIONSHIPS

What is the most important piece of any healthy relationship?

Maybe the first thing you thought of was love or trust or selflessness. But let us suggest an answer that is even deeper: *truth*.

Relationships simply cannot exist without truth. If I lie to you about who I am, then you don't know the real me. We can only know each other to the degree that we are honest with one another. The root problem in our relationships is that we are all more dishonest than we think we are. We hide the bad parts of our lives and we project the impressive things. Social media only makes this problem worse.

We are going to look at two areas where we struggle to be honest in our relationships: **telling the truth about ourselves** and **telling the truth about others**. Both are necessary if we want real relationships.

TELLING THE TRUTH ABOUT OURSELVES

First, we are tempted to avoid telling the truth about ourselves because we don't want people to know us as we really are. We want to appear a certain way—to be known as a certain kind of person. So we create an "image" for ourselves. Author Brennan Manning refers to this image as "the impostor":

[We] present a perfect image to the public so that everybody will admire us and nobody will know us. . . . The
false self causes us to live in a world of delusion. The
impostor is a liar.[5]

Christians are good at being impostors. It's exactly what Adam and
Eve did in the garden of Eden. When God created them, they were
"naked, and they felt no shame" (Genesis 2:25). But once they sinned,
they became aware of their nakedness and "sewed fig leaves together"
(Genesis 3:7) to cover up the shame they now felt. Then when God
came to the garden, they hid from him out of fear and shame. They
tried everything they could think of to avoid honestly owning up to
what they had done. Their sin damaged their relationships with each
other and with God; their dishonesty about their sin made the damage
worse. They had started withholding things from each other and from
God.

We've been doing the same thing ever since: hiding our sins and mistakes to make ourselves look better.

This dishonesty about ourselves is one of the main causes of shallow
community. The apostle John calls it "walking in darkness." And his
remedy is *truth*—or, as he puts it, "walking in the light":

God is light, and in him is no darkness at all. If we say
we have fellowship with him while we walk in darkness,
we lie and do not practice the truth. But if we walk in the
light, as he is in the light, we have fellowship with one
another, and the blood of Jesus his Son cleanses us from
all sin. If we say we have no sin, we deceive ourselves, and
the truth is not in us. If we confess our sins, he is faithful
and just to forgive us our sins and to cleanse us from all
unrighteousness. (1 John 1:5–9 ESV)

"If we walk in the light, as God is in the light, we have fellowship with
one another." In other words, when we are open and honest, we have

true community. We have real relationship. We're not pretending, hiding, covering up. You know the real me, and I know the real you. And that's a good recipe for genuine friendship.

But *how* can we consistently walk in the light? What gives us the freedom to live in honesty and truth with one another? It's the gospel. The gospel tells us the truth about ourselves: We sin, and we cannot fix ourselves. But "the blood of Jesus . . . cleanses us from all sin" (1 John 1:7 ESV). Jesus has given us his perfect record, and God accepts us and adopts us into his family. We are secure in his love. When we really grasp the love and security God gives us, we can be confident rather than fearful. We don't need to hide who we are or worry about what other people think. In Jesus, our shame is taken away, and our struggle for righteousness and identity is resolved. We are God's beloved children, and nothing can change that!

The confidence that comes to us through the gospel makes it possible for us to be truthful about ourselves. And this truthfulness makes it possible for us to experience the kind of honest community we long for.

So when you find yourself afraid of what people would think if they knew the real truth about you, remind yourself that you don't need to keep up a false image of yourself and protect it at all costs by hiding or pretending. You don't have to struggle to keep up appearances. The good news of the gospel is that your identity is in Christ, not in what people think of you. And your righteousness comes from Christ, not your good behavior or reputation. Jesus gives you a new identity and a righteousness you did not earn on your own. They are yours by grace. And because you didn't earn them, you can't lose them! You can find peace in the identity and righteousness that Jesus provides.

SPEAKING THE TRUTH TO OTHERS

Hiding our true selves and putting up a false image is the first way we are tempted to be dishonest in our relationships; a second way we are tempted to be dishonest is not telling others the truth about themselves when hearing it would really help them.

The fact is, we do not see ourselves accurately. We think more highly of ourselves than we ought to, and we think less of ourselves than we ought to. We all have areas of sin and weakness in our lives. And we all have blind spots. This is why we are commanded to speak the truth in love to one another (Ephesians 4:15). We need the insight of others who know us and care about us. They can help us see the truth about what we've been thinking or doing. Then we can ask God to forgive us, work in our hearts, and lead us back into the light.

Speaking truth to one another can take many forms: encouraging, teaching, warning, challenging, confronting, etc. But the point is always "speaking the truth *in love*" (Ephesians 4:15, emphasis added). Loving people means truly wanting what is good for them. So relying on the Holy Spirit, we speak truth to build people up in their faith and help them walk in the light. If truth-telling is motivated by pride or defensiveness or anger, it will only hurt people and damage relationships. But when we speak with kindness and humility, we reflect the love and grace God has shown us—and we remind the other person of the love and grace God has for them.

When the gospel of grace is believed, reflected on, and talked about in community, that brings about life-changing honesty. In such a community, people will learn to find their identity in Christ and not in the approval of others; self-righteousness will give way to the righteousness we receive by faith in Jesus; and people will be loved as they really are, yet also helped to grow to be more like Jesus. It will be a community of light, truth, goodness, and beauty, where the glory of God is on display to the world.

Isn't that the kind of community you want? It all starts with you and me walking in the light.

DISCUSSION

What idea stood out to you most in this article?

Why do you think it feels safer and easier to show others an image rather than the truth about ourselves?

Do you find it is hard to encourage and teach others? Why, or why not?

Do you find it hard to warn or confront people about possible areas of sin? Why, or why not?

What do you think would happen in this community if we were more honest about ourselves and about others?

SPEAKING THE TRUTH IN LOVE

We've been talking about two kinds of honesty: telling the truth about ourselves and telling the truth to others. This exercise is designed to help us grow by investigating why we find it hard to be honest and by encouraging us to embrace the freedom that comes from the good news of the gospel.

1. Choose the statement below that most resonates with your own struggle to be honest:

   ☐ There are some things about me I'd rather not share with others.

   ☐ I'm not sure how people would respond if they knew "the real me."

   ☐ People aren't always trustworthy. If they knew the whole truth about me, I'm worried about how they could slander, gossip, or embarrass me.

   ☐ When my friends are talking in demeaning or sinful ways about others, I often struggle to speak up.

   ☐ When someone in our small group shares a viewpoint that doesn't line up with what is true or good, I prefer to let it go instead of engaging the person in further conversation.

   ☐ I often see something in someone else that I appreciate or admire, but it feels awkward to say something… so I don't say anything.

2. Read the verses below; circle one or two that speak to your situation.

- "Be careful then, dear brothers and sisters. Make sure that your own hearts are not evil and unbelieving, turning you away from the living God. You must warn each other every day, while it is still 'today,' so that none of you will be deceived by sin and hardened against God. For if we are faithful to the end, trusting God just as firmly as when we first believed, we will share in all that belongs to Christ" (Hebrews 3:12–14 NLT).

- "Let us consider how we may spur one another on toward love and good deeds, not giving up meeting together, as some are in the habit of doing, but encouraging one another—and all the more as you see the Day approaching" (Hebrews 10:24–25).

- "Be like-minded, be sympathetic, love one another, be compassionate and humble" (1 Peter 3:8).

- "If we say we have fellowship with him while we walk in darkness, we lie and do not practice the truth. But if we walk in the light, as he is in the light, we have fellowship with one another, and the blood of Jesus his Son cleanses us from all sin. If we say we have no sin, we deceive ourselves, and the truth is not in us. If we confess our sins, he is faithful and just to forgive us our sins and to cleanse us from all unrighteousness" (1 John 1:6–9 ESV).

- "So do not be afraid of them, for there is nothing concealed that will not be disclosed, or hidden that will not be made known. What I tell you in the dark, speak in the daylight; what is whispered in your ear, proclaim from the roofs. Do not be afraid of those who kill the body but cannot kill the soul. Rather, be afraid of the One who can destroy both soul and body in hell. Are not two sparrows sold for a penny? Yet not one of them will fall to the ground outside your Father's care. And even the very hairs of your head are all numbered. So don't be afraid; you are worth more than many sparrows. Whoever acknowledges me before others, I will also acknowledge before my Father in heaven. But

whoever disowns me before others, I will disown before my
Father in heaven" (Matthew 10:26–33).

- "Therefore each of you must put off falsehood and speak truthfully to your neighbor, for we are all members of one body"
  (Ephesians 4:25).

3. What truth in these verses do you see yourself not really believing
   (actually living as though it's true)?

4. If you really lived out of your union with Jesus Christ—in other
   words, if you really believed that you belong to him, and that his
   Word is true—how might that free you for greater honesty?

If you wish, share your answers with the group at the end of the exercise time.

WRAP-UP

Ask any remaining questions, make final comments, and pray together,
asking the Holy Spirit to help us remember the truths we have learned
so that we will grow in being honest with one another in a loving,
humble way.

7

LESSON

A JOYFUL COMMUNITY

BIG IDEA

In the last lesson, we learned about how the gospel of grace makes it possible for us to be honest about ourselves and one another. In this lesson, we'll look at another result of grasping the gospel of grace: joy. God is full of joy and sent Jesus so that his joy could be in us. One aspect of the gospel that we really need to understand is that God does two things in every person he rescues. First, he *justifies* us: On the cross Jesus took the punishment that we deserve because of our sin, and through faith in Jesus, God credits us with his righteousness. The second part is called *sanctification*. Whoever is justified by faith also receives the Holy Spirit, who is at work to make us more like Jesus. Understanding the relationship between justification and sanctification will help us experience joy in Christ.

BIBLE CONVERSATION

This week you will read a few verses from the New Testament, beginning with a short parable Jesus told.

Read Matthew 13:44 aloud. As you read this verse, focus on the concept of joy.

Then discuss these questions together:

- What causes the man in the parable to have joy?

- What does he do because of his joy?

- How would you describe joy? How do you think it is similar to or different from the way we normally think about happiness or satisfaction?

Now read these two short passages: 1 Thessalonians 5:23–24 and 2 Corinthians 3:17–18. As you read, notice what each one says about *sanctification*, God's process of changing us to be like Jesus.

Then discuss these questions together:

- What does sanctification (spiritual growth) look like?

- How does sanctification happen in our lives?

A JOYFUL COMMUNITY

Everyone wants to be happy,[6] and almost everything we do is in pursuit of happiness. This desire makes sense because we were made to delight and rejoice in God and his works (Genesis 2:15-16). Sin is simply an attempt to find happiness apart from God (Genesis 3:6-7), a quest that is ultimately futile. Jesus came to bring us the joy of our salvation. One of the last things he said to his disciples was, "these things I have spoken to you, that my joy may be in you, and that your joy may be full" (John 15:11 ESV).

There is a me-centered kind of happiness that is all about gratifying my own desires. But the Bible tells us that true happiness is all about enjoying the presence and power of God in our lives. The Psalms express this kind of happiness:

- "In your presence there is fullness of joy; at your right hand are pleasures forevermore" (Psalm 16:11 ESV).

- "Taste and see that the LORD is good; blessed [happy!] is the one who takes refuge in him!" (Psalm 34:8).

- "Take delight in the LORD, and he will give you the desires of your heart" (Psalm 37:4).

There is also a superficial kind of happiness that downplays negative emotions and tries to "keep things positive." But the Bible is real about the hard things in life, and the New Testament even speaks of having joy in the midst of sorrow and suffering:

- "We rejoice in hope of the glory of God. Not only that, but *we rejoice in our sufferings…*" (Romans 5:2–3 ESV, emphasis added).

- "You became imitators of us and of the Lord, for you welcomed the message *in the midst of severe suffering with the joy* given by the Holy Spirit" (1 Thessalonians 1:6, emphasis added).

JOY IN THE GOSPEL AND THE HOLY SPIRIT

Christian joy is a supernatural happiness that comes from believing the gospel and experiencing the power of the Holy Spirit in our lives. Notice how the Bible connects these two things to our joy:

- "Though you have not seen him, you love him; and even though you do not see him now, you **believe** in him and are **filled with an inexpressible and glorious joy**…" (1 Peter 1:8, emphasis added).

- "May the God of hope **fill you with all joy** and peace as you **trust** in him, so that you may overflow with hope by **the power of the Holy Spirit**" (Romans 15:13, emphasis added).

Our joy is rooted in the unchanging truth of the gospel and the ongoing ministry of the Holy Spirit. When we do not feel joyful, it is because we have forgotten the gospel and become focused on ourselves rather than dependent on the Spirit.

How does this happen? How do we forget the gospel and become self-reliant? One way we do this is by mixing up justification and sanctification.

UNDERSTANDING JUSTIFICATION AND SANCTIFICATION

Justification is a legal word that means we have been declared righteous. God—who is the ultimate Judge—not only pardons our guilt but also declares us righteous in Christ. This is the amazing exchange of the gospel: "God made him who had no sin to be sin for us, so that in him we might become the righteousness of God" (2 Corinthians 5:21). Whoever believes in Jesus has been justified: "Since we have been justified through faith [past tense, once and for all], we [now] have peace with God" (Romans 5:1).

Sanctification is the process of spiritual growth and maturity. God declares us *righteous* (that is our legal standing), and then he makes us increasingly righteous in our actual lives. The Holy Spirit is always at work to transform us and make us more like Jesus. Our part in the process is to seek God and yield to the work of the Spirit. If we keep in step with the Spirit, we will not give in to our selfish desires, and we will experience the fruit of the Spirit, which includes joy! (see Galatians 5:16–24).

Justification and sanctification are both gifts from God. It's important to remember how these gifts work, though, because if we get the order wrong, we can get discouraged and lose our joy.

We must always start with the fact of justification. It is done, finished, secure. Sometimes when we are struggling spiritually, we don't feel justified. We don't *feel* like God forgives and accepts us. Likewise, if we think we are "doing well" spiritually, we feel justified, as if God accepts us based on our performance. Either way, we end up basing what we believe about our justification on how our sanctification is going. When we do that, our joy will rise and fall on our feelings about how we think we are doing.

LASTING JOY

So how do we experience lasting joy? By rooting ourselves in the truth of justification by faith. This is what Paul does in Romans (notice the order in this passage):

- "Therefore, since *we have been justified* by faith, we have peace with God through our Lord Jesus Christ" (Romans 5:1 ESV, emphasis added). This is our foundation every day. It is unchanging.

- "Through [Jesus] we have also obtained access by faith into this grace in which we stand, and we rejoice in hope of the glory of God" (Romans 5:2 ESV). No matter how we think we are doing, we stand in grace, which gives us confidence that God will complete his work in our lives.

- "Not only that, but we rejoice in our sufferings, knowing that suffering produces endurance, and endurance produces character, and character produces hope" (Romans 5:3–4 ESV). Because we have peace with God and stand in grace, we can have joy even in our sufferings. God uses the hard things in our lives to make us more like Jesus.

- "Hope does not put us to shame, because God's love has been poured into our hearts through the Holy Spirit who has been given to us" (Romans 5:5 ESV). The Holy Spirit reminds us of God's justifying love—"that while we were still sinners, Christ died for us" (Romans 5:8 ESV).

Relying completely on Christ's work on my behalf is essential to experiencing deep and lasting joy. When my sanctification is slow and my struggles against sin are intense, I'm still joyful because Jesus is my righteousness! When I am growing and doing great things for God, I'm joyful because Jesus is my righteousness! (See Luke 10:20.)

Either way, I am not motivated by *pride* or *fear* (thinking that I can or must earn God's approval). Instead, I'm motivated by *love* for God, knowing that he loves me and has declared me righteous, once and for all.

When we keep our eyes on the truth of justification, we become a gospel-centered community that radiates joy.

DISCUSSION

What stood out to you in the article? Anything particularly interesting or challenging?

What do you think it means to be happy?

In what ways have you tried to pursue happiness apart from God?

Why is true happiness rooted in justification by faith?

HAPPINESS KILLERS

Let's talk about what steals our happiness. These are all things that can take our eyes off of what God has done for us and turn our focus in on self. Take a few minutes to read through these six descriptions. Check anything that you identify with. Then use the questions below to share your takeaways.

☐ **Entitlement** is the belief that we deserve certain things or rights. When we feel entitled to things that don't come through for us, it kills our joy, because our hope is misplaced. Joy flows from a heart that trusts in God's promises. *What do you feel entitled to (for example, respect, comfort, privilege, a certain financial status)?*

☐ **Comparison** is measuring ourselves against others. So, if someone has more than me, or seems happier than me, or is more successful than me, I feel cheated or envious. Comparison kills our happiness because joy flows from a heart that is content. *What area of your life are you prone to compare against others'?*

☐ **A hurried life** means we are always on the go, never feeling like we have the time to slow down and reflect. Happiness gets pushed out and replaced by busyness, activity, and productivity. Joy flows from a heart that experiences rest in God. *What areas of your life feel hurried? Where do you sense a lack of rest in God?*

☐ **Works-righteousness** means basing our sense of value or belonging on what we do (our good deeds, behaviors, successes, and spiritual practices). Joy flows from a heart that is rooted in grace. *In what ways do you feel like you have to prove yourself to God?*

☐ **Self-absorption** is an unhealthy focus on one's own emotions, thoughts, interests, or situation. Joy flows from a heart that is focused on God and others. *Where do you see the pull toward self-absorption in your life?*

☐ **Spiritual funk** is the state of feeling distant from God. When we do not deal with sin, when we are not spending time in God's Word, and when we isolate ourselves from others, we close ourselves off from the work of the Spirit. *In what ways do you feel distant from God? Why do you think that is?*

SHARING QUESTIONS:

1. What did you *most* identify with in these descriptions?

2. How does that keep you from remembering that you have been justified by faith?

3. How does the gospel set us free from these things?

WRAP-UP

Ask any remaining questions, make final comments, and pray together, asking the Holy Spirit to help us cling to the truth that we have been justified by faith and to fill us with joy because of this gracious gift.

A COMMUNITY ON A MISSION

BIG IDEA

Since Lesson 4, we have been exploring some of the features of a biblical community: grace, humility, honesty, and joy. In this last lesson, we're going to consider one final characteristic of a gospel-centered community: mission. Christian community always has an outward face, *moving toward others as God has moved toward us.* We are called to leave our comfortable spaces and social circles to move toward people who don't know Christ, becoming friends with them, loving them, and inviting them into the community of faith. The Father sent the Son, the Son sent the Spirit, and the Spirit sends everyone who believes in Jesus. As we are changed by the Holy Spirit through the gospel, we are a "sent" people, on mission together!

BIBLE CONVERSATION

In this lesson, we will be looking at what it means to live "on mission"—loving and sharing the gospel with people around us who don't know Jesus. These two passages will help us think about what that means.

Read 2 Corinthians 5:14–20 aloud. As you read, look for what the passage says about sharing the gospel.

Then discuss these questions together:

- This passage says that Jesus died for us and that by his death God has "reconciled us to himself" (verse 18).

    - What does it mean for someone to be reconciled to someone else?

    - Why did we need to be reconciled to God?

- What work have we been given now that we have been reconciled to God? (verses 18–20)

    - What does an ambassador do?

    - What do you think it might look like to be one of "Christ's ambassadors" (verse 20)?

8

A MISSIONAL COMMUNITY

Maybe you've been in a stadium to see one of your favorite performers. Do you remember the feeling you had when the singer stopped singing and the crowd took over, belting the lyrics together at the top of their lungs? Or maybe you've seen a victory parade, like when a sports team wins the championship and everyone is wearing the team colors and cheering together when the players go by.

Moments like these give us a taste of the ultimate joy and unity God's people will experience at the end of history. Revelation 7 gives us a glimpse of that day:

> After this I looked, and there before me was a great
> multitude that no one could count, from every nation,
> tribe, people and language, standing before the throne
> and before the Lamb. They were wearing white robes and
> were holding palm branches in their hands. And they
> cried out in a loud voice:
>> "Salvation belongs to our God,
>> who sits on the throne,
>> and to the Lamb." (Revelation 7:9–10)

God's mission is to redeem a people from every corner of the earth, so great in number that they can't be counted, and so joyful that they can't stop singing. Here is the incredible thing: The way God accomplishes his mission is through us! Through our witness, people can hear the gospel and become part of God's family. They can experience real community now and someday be part of the ultimate community gathered around the throne of God. A gospel-centered community is on mission together.

WHAT DO YOU THINK OF WHEN YOU HEAR THE WORD *MISSION*?

When you hear the word *mission*, certain ideas might pop up in your head.

It might make you think of *missionaries* who go to other nations to share the gospel. But that is just one form of mission. In reality, *all* Christians are missionaries, regardless of where they live or whether they travel long distances. If you have put your faith in Jesus, then God is sending you as his ambassador to share the good news about Jesus. Wherever you are—school, neighborhood, sports teams—that is your mission field.

Mission might also make you think of certain "evangelistic" activities that we do at designated times, like a special outreach event at church. But mission isn't just an activity we do or an event we hold. It is a way of life. As we go, the Holy Spirit leads us into various situations and conversations. He gives us compassion for others, and he gives us words to speak to them. We move toward people with good news, and we invite them into community so they can experience the love of Christ through his people.

We can learn from the example of the early Christians in Acts. They were just doing life together, and many others were drawn in by what they saw and heard: "Every day they continued to meet together in the temple courts. They broke bread in their homes and ate together with glad and sincere hearts, praising God and enjoying the favor of all the people. And the Lord added to their number daily those who were being saved" (Acts 2:46–47). The mission of God goes forward through the people of God, wherever they are and whatever they're doing, even if it's just normal, everyday stuff.

Maybe the word *mission* makes you a little nervous. Perhaps you've gotten the sense that God has given some people the gift of evangelism, but you don't see yourself as one of them. It is true that God gives each person their own unique set of gifts. But we are all called to love and serve people around us and share the gospel with them, using the gifts God has given us in the situations where God had placed us.

WHAT DOES MISSION LOOK LIKE?

So what does a missional *community* look like? There are hundreds of ways to answer that question, but let's focus on one simple idea: *Mission means moving toward others as God has moved toward us.*

Mission means moving toward others. Often we do our "Christian" things at church or youth group, and we hope non-Christians will show up and want to learn about Jesus. It is great when people show up, but Jesus shows us a better way. He comes to us. If God had waited for us to come to him, we'd still be stuck in our sin and brokenness. But he made the first move, stepping out of heaven and into our world: "The Word became human and made his home among us" (John 1:14 NLT). The message of the gospel is that God moved toward us while we were running in the opposite direction! Now God calls us to move toward others in the same way. Instead of waiting for others to come to us, we take the initiative and go to them. In our everyday life—studying with others, playing sports, or just talking—we remember that we are ambassadors of Jesus. We represent him in our words and actions. We talk about our faith in the "real world."

Mission means inviting others in. God moved toward us to redeem us, to make us part of his family. Throughout the Bible we see God's constant concern for people who are strangers, outsiders, and foreigners. He instructed his people: "The foreigner residing among you must be treated as your native-born. Love them as yourself, for you were foreigners in Egypt. I am the LORD your God" (Leviticus 19:34). Like our Father in heaven, we long to see strangers become friends. We long to see those who are separated from God become reconciled to him. So we do *everything* in a way that will make people who don't know Jesus feel welcome. We love people and we work for their good. We invite them into our life and community. This could mean inviting them to church, to our house for dinner, or just to hang out with our Christian friends. These are all opportunities for people to hear the gospel and experience its power firsthand.

Mission means relying on God's power. We can make plans and work hard to carry them out. But if we really want to bless others for the long haul, we can't rely on our own feelings, plans, and efforts. We must rely on God's power. Reaching out to others, loving others, helping others—that's not easy. We'll get tired. We'll be uncomfortable sometimes. From time to time, we'll get annoyed. We just can't do it on our own. So how do we rely on God's power? First, we continually remember and rejoice in what Jesus has done for us (Luke 10:20). Second, we ask God to open doors for the gospel in our everyday activities and to give us courage to walk through them with wisdom and grace (Colossians 4:2–6). Finally, we trust God for the results. Only he can change people's hearts (1 Corinthians 3:7)!

A gospel-centered community is a community of people who are growing in seeing their lives as part of God's mission. They are moving toward others as God has moved toward them. They are looking for opportunities to bless and serve others so that more and more people might gain hope and salvation in Jesus. They understand that mission flows out of hearts changed by God's grace. And they can see by faith that the love they show people around them is part of God's great mission throughout history, a mission that will reach its glorious finale in a gathering of worshippers "from every nation, tribe, people and language" (Revelation 7:9).

DISCUSSION

What was new to you in this discussion of mission? How does this compare with how you have thought about mission in the past?

"Mission means moving toward others as God has moved toward us." What do you find **exciting** about that? What do you find **challenging** about it?

What do you think it would look like for you to be more "missional" in your life?

How can we share in the mission together?

LIVING ON MISSION

This week's exercise will help you think about mission opportunities in your life.

First, review this statement that summarizes what the article said about mission: ***Mission means moving toward others as God has moved toward us.***

Then answer the questions below individually. You will be asked about things you plan to pray about and do. Remember that you will need God's help to do them, and remember that if you forget or mess up, God loves you and gives you more grace.

Finally, discuss the questions as a group. In your discussion, be careful to be gracious, encouraging, and truthful, and to listen carefully to others. Think about how you can encourage one another as you seek to live out the things you are discussing.

CONSIDER YOUR RELATIONSHIPS

- Who are some non-Christians friends you would like to move toward? What might that look like?

- What are some ways you could invite some of your Christian and non-Christian friends into the same space (common interests, social gatherings, an event, etc.)?

Write down one thing you will pray about and try to put into action in the next two weeks.

CONSIDER YOUR PRAYERS

- Do you pray for the people in your life who do not know Jesus?

- Do you pray about God's big mission where you live and around the world?

Write down one thing to add to your prayer life.

CONSIDER YOUR LANGUAGE AND ATTITUDE

- Do you speak positively about those who don't know Christ? Do you have gospel humility—admitting your own weaknesses, not taking yourself too seriously, and not being defensive or rude toward people who don't share your beliefs? Are non-Christians glad to know you, even if they don't believe the gospel?

- Do you speak up for people in your community who may otherwise go unnoticed?

Write down one way you will pray for God's help to grow in this area.

CONSIDER THE GROUP'S ACTIVITY AND PRESENCE

- Are there ways we can be more involved in the community around us?

- Are there ways our group can be more involved in the mission of God to other places and cultures?

Write down one idea you want to follow up on.

Take a few minutes to share your ideas with the group, if you wish.

WRAP-UP

Ask any remaining questions, make final comments, and pray together, asking the Holy Spirit to give members of the group hearts that want to move toward people and opportunities to do so. Pray that you would encourage one another as you seek to be on mission.

LEADER'S NOTES

GOSPEL OVERVIEW

The study you are about to begin aims to help you live a gospel-centered life in a gospel-centered community. The obvious question is, What exactly is "the gospel"? That's a question we should clear up before going any further. Though many people are familiar with the word *gospel*, we're often fuzzy about its content.

Many popular "gospel presentations" boil the gospel message down to three or four points. These simple summaries can be very helpful. But a richer way to understand the gospel is as a *story*—the true Story that speaks to our purest aspirations and deepest longings. This Great Story has four chapters.

Creation: The World We Were Made For

The Story begins, not with us, but with God. Deep down, we have a sense that this is true. We sense that we are important—that there is something dignified, majestic, and eternal about humanity. But we also know that something (or Someone) greater than us exists.

The Bible tells us that this Someone is the one infinite, eternal, and unchanging God who created all things out of nothing (Genesis 1:1–31). This one God exists in three persons—Father, Son, and Holy Spirit (Matthew 28:19). Because God is three-in-one, a community unto himself, he didn't create the world because he *needed* something—be it relationship, worship, or glory. Rather, he created out of the overflow of his own perfect love, goodness, and glory. God made human beings in his image (Genesis 1:27), which is what gives us our dignity and value. He also made us *human*, which means we are created beings, dependent on our Creator. We were made to worship, enjoy, love, and serve him, not ourselves.

In God's original creation, everything was good. The world existed in perfect peace, stability, harmony, and wholeness.

Fall: The Corruption of Everything

God created us to worship, enjoy, love, and serve him. But rather than live under God's authority, humanity turned away from God in sinful rebellion (Genesis 3:1–7; Isaiah 53:6). Our disobedience plunged the whole world into the darkness and chaos of sin. Though some good remains, the wholeness and harmony of God's original creation is shattered.

As a result, all human beings are sinners (Ephesians 2:1–3). We often excuse our sin by claiming that we're "not that bad"—after all, we can always find someone worse than we are! But this excuse only reveals our shallow view of sin. Sin is not primarily an *action*; it's the way our hearts and minds pull away from God. Sin is manifested in our pride, our selfishness, our independence, and our lack of love for God and others. Sometimes sin is very obvious and external; other times it's hidden and internal. But "all have sinned and fall short of the glory of God" (Romans 3:23).

Sin brings two terrible consequences into our lives. First, *sin enslaves us* (Romans 6:17–18). When we turn *from* God, we turn *to* other things to find our life, our identity, our meaning, and our happiness.

These things become substitute gods—what the Bible calls idols—and they enslave us, demanding our time, our energy, our loyalty, our money—everything we are and have. They begin to rule over our lives and hearts. This is why the Bible describes sin as something that "masters" us (Romans 6:14). Sin causes us to "serve created things rather than the Creator" (Romans 1:25).

Second, *sin brings condemnation*. We're not just enslaved by our sin; we're *guilty* because of it. We stand condemned before the Judge of heaven and earth. "The wages of sin is death" (Romans 6:23). We are under a death sentence for our cosmic treason against the holiness and justice of God. His righteous anger toward sin stands over us (Nahum 1:2; John 3:36).

Redemption: Jesus Comes to Save Us

Every good story has a hero. And the hero of the Gospel Story is Jesus. Humanity needs a Savior, a Deliverer to free us from the bondage and condemnation of sin and to restore the world to its original good. This Rescuer must be *truly human* in order to pay the debt we owe to God. But he can't be *merely human* because he must conquer sin. We need a Substitute—one who can live the life of obedience we've failed to live, and who can stand in our place to bear the punishment we deserve for our disobedience and sin.

This is why God sent Jesus into the world to be our substitute (1 John 4:14). The Bible teaches that Jesus was fully God—the second person of the Trinity—and also fully human. He was born to a human mother, lived a real flesh-and-blood existence, and died a brutal death on a Roman cross outside Jerusalem. Jesus lived a life of perfect obedience to God (Hebrews 4:15), making him the only person in history who did not deserve judgment. But on the cross, he took our place, dying for our sin. He received the condemnation and death we deserve so that, when we put our trust in him, we can receive the blessing and life he deserves (2 Corinthians 5:21).

Not only did Jesus die in our place, he rose from death, displaying his victory over sin, death, and hell. His resurrection is a turning point in history; the Bible calls it the "first fruits"—the first evidence—of the cosmic renewal God is bringing (1 Corinthians 15:20–28). One of the greatest promises in the Bible is Revelation 21:5: "Behold, I am making all things new" (ESV). All that was lost, broken, and corrupted in the fall will ultimately be put right. Redemption doesn't simply mean the salvation of individual souls; it means the restoration of all creation back to its original good.

A New People: The Story Continues

So how do we become a part of the Story? How do we experience God's salvation personally and become agents of his redemption in the world? By faith, or trust (Ephesians 2:8–9). What does that mean? We trust a taxi driver when we count on him to get us to our destination. We trust a doctor when we agree with her diagnosis and entrust ourselves to her care. And we trust in Jesus Christ when we admit our sin, receive his gracious forgiveness, and rest entirely in Jesus for our acceptance before God. Faith is like getting in the taxi or going under the surgeon's knife. It's a restful, whole-hearted commitment of the self to Jesus (Psalm 31:14–15). This is what it means to believe the gospel.

When we trust in Jesus, we are released from sin's condemnation *and* from its bondage. We are free to say "no" to sin and "yes" to God. We are free to die to ourselves and live for Christ and his purposes. We are free to work for justice in the world. We are free to stop living for our own glory and start living for the glory of God (1 Corinthians 10:31). We are free to love God and others in the way we live, which is the particular focus of this study.

God has promised that Jesus will return to finally judge sin and make all things new. Until then, he is gathering to himself a people "from every nation, tribe, people and language" (Revelation 7:9). As part of that called-and-sent people, we have the privilege of joining him in his mission (Matthew 28:18–20) as individuals and as part of his spiritual family. By grace, we can enjoy God, live life for his glory, serve humanity, and make his gospel known to others through our words and actions.

This is the good news—the True Story—of the gospel.

LESSON 1: THE CHALLENGE OF COMMUNITY

ORIENTATION *(FIRST SESSION ONLY)*

Before beginning this first lesson, you'll want to offer the group a quick orientation to the study.

Today we're starting a study that will help us think about how the gospel affects relationships and community. Each week, we'll talk about some Bible verses, read a short article, discuss the ideas it presents, and do an exercise to help us apply what we're learning. Because we're trying to build community, we want to listen well to one another, and when we speak, we want to speak honestly but also kindly, interacting in a way that's loving and encouraging.

LESSON OVERVIEW

I. BIG IDEA	Read (or ask a volunteer to read) the Big Idea aloud (2 min)
II. BIBLE CONVERSATION	Read and talk about the passages (10 min)
III. ARTICLE	Read "The Challenge of Community" together (10 min)
IV. DISCUSSION	Process the concepts together (15 min)
V. EXERCISE	Apply the concepts using the "Considering My Connections" exercise (15 min)
VI. WRAP-UP	Share final thoughts and pray (5 min)

BIBLE CONVERSATION *(10 min)*

The purpose of the Bible conversation portion of the lesson is to get the group thinking about community in biblical terms. The goal is not to say everything there is to say about the verses you read. The goal is simply to get the conversation going in a way that gives a biblical foundation for the concepts that are the focus of the lesson.

In the first passage for this lesson, Psalm 142:1–5, David cries out to the Lord, who he knows is his refuge. But David has no human companionship or support: "no one is concerned for me" (verse 4). In contrast, in the second passage, 1 Corinthians 12:12–27, Paul gives us a beautiful picture of the unity and diversity of Christian community: We are the body of Christ, in which every part is needed and supported.

SETUP We are going to talk about *community*—what it means and what challenges it brings. The two Bible readings will help us start to think about our need for community and about what community can look like in Christ.

READ AND ASK *First reading: Have someone read Psalm 142:1–5 aloud. Then answer the questions.*

Second reading: Have someone read 1 Corinthians 12:12–27 aloud. Then answer the questions.

TRANSITION TO ARTICLE The passages we read got us thinking about our need for community and about what a community built on faith in Jesus can look like. But even though we need relationships, they can be hard. The article we're about to read explores some of the challenges of community. Let's read it aloud together, taking turns at the paragraph breaks. If you prefer not to read, just say "Pass," and the next person will pick up reading. When we're done, we'll have some discussion questions to help us process what we just read.

ARTICLE *(10 min)*

There are two reasons for reading an article together: (1) to explain key concepts so that everyone in your group has a common understanding and vocabulary, and (2) to provide a focus for conversation. We want to help your group learn how to talk about the gospel in relation to their actual lives. In many cases people do not talk about what Jesus did for them or what it means for their lives because they simply don't have much to say. The article gives them things to talk about and language to use to express their thoughts.

READ THE ARTICLE TOGETHER *Ask the group to turn to the article "The Challenge of Community" and read it aloud together.*

TRANSITION TO DISCUSSION Okay, there's a lot to think about here. We'll look at the discussion questions in the book to help us out, but if you have any other questions you'd like to ask or comments you'd like to make as we go along, feel free.

DISCUSSION *(15 min)*

These discussion questions are aimed at helping the group make connections between the article and their own lives. You may want to ask follow-up questions as the discussion goes along.

Read each discussion question aloud, and have participants discuss it.

Note: Allow some time after you read each question for participants to think about it. Pauses can feel uncomfortable, but they are helpful for those who need to process before they are ready to speak.

TRANSITION TO EXERCISE This is really good. We're talking about some challenging things, and in the next session we'll explore the roots of those challenges. But for now we're going to end with an exercise that will help us think about the relationships we have.

EXERCISE *(15 min)*

SETUP *Read the introduction and instructions for the exercise.*

DO THE EXERCISE *Give participants several minutes to complete the exercise on their own.*

SHARE   *Once participants have worked through the exercise, give them the opportunity to share if they wish. Especially this first week, you might want to remind them to really listen to one another.*

TRANSITION TO WRAP-UP   That's great! Thank you for sharing. Before we wrap up, does anyone have any more questions or comments?

WRAP-UP *(5 min)*

Okay, let's wrap up!

Pray as a group, asking that in the next several weeks God would use the things you are studying in the lives of each person and in the group as a whole. If time is short, you can pray (or ask if one person would volunteer to pray).

LESSON 2: THE BACKSTORY

LESSON OVERVIEW

I. BIG IDEA   Read (or ask a volunteer to read) the Big Idea aloud (2 min)

II. BIBLE CONVERSATION   Read and talk about the passages (10 min)

III. ARTICLE   Read "The Backstory" together (10 min)

IV. DISCUSSION   Process the concepts together (15 min)

V. EXERCISE   Apply the concepts using exercise "The Self and Others" (15 min)

VI. WRAP-UP   Share final thoughts and pray (5 min)

BIBLE CONVERSATION *(10 min)*

The passages for this lesson are foundational to our understanding of humanity, so they are also foundational to our understanding of humans in community. The verses from Genesis 1 tell us that God created humans in his image. The article will build on this to show that because God is relational, humans are too. In Genesis 1:31 we read that God's creation is "very good." But the passage from Genesis 3 shows us the fall, when Adam and Eve choose their own way rather than God's. Their actions harm their relationships with God and with each other.

It won't be possible to discuss every aspect of these passages. The goal is for the group to understand these two bedrock truths: Humans are made in God's image and therefore reflect him; and humans rejected God and his ways, with painful effects that are still with us today.

SETUP   We are going to read two passages from Genesis, the first book of the Bible. These passages will help us understand what it means to be human and how we humans relate to God and one another.

READ AND ASK   *First reading: Have someone read Genesis 1:26–27, 31 aloud. Then answer the questions.*

Second reading: Have someone read Genesis 3:2–13 aloud. Then answer the questions.

TRANSITION TO ARTICLE   The passages we just read explain a lot about human nature. The article we are going to read makes connections between what happened back in Genesis and what we experience in our relationships today. Let's read the article together and then talk about it.

ARTICLE *(10 min)*

On the surface, the Bible passages for this lesson may seem simple. But they have a lot of power to explain what we see and experience in our world and relationships. The article will help participants connect the dots between Genesis and our lives in the twenty-first century.

READ THE ARTICLE TOGETHER   *Ask the group to turn to the article "The Backstory" and read it aloud together. Change readers at the paragraph breaks.*

DISCUSSION *(15 min)*

Read each discussion question aloud, and have participants discuss it.

TRANSITION TO EXERCISE   We've read some hard things about what people are like, but we've also gotten to see why there's hope! The exercise we're about to do will help us see areas where we're tempted to be self-focused and get us to think about alternatives that can help us build good community.

EXERCISE *(15 min)*

SETUP   *Read the introduction (or explain it in your own words), and go over the instructions for the exercise.*

DO THE EXERCISE   *Give participants several minutes to complete the exercise on their own.*

SHARE   *Once participants have worked through the exercise, give them the opportunity to share if they wish.*

TRANSITION TO WRAP-UP   I know that was a lot to think about. Thank you for your thoughts! Before we wrap up, does anyone have any more questions or comments?

WRAP-UP *(5 min)*

Pray as a group, asking that in the next several weeks God would use the things you are studying in the lives of each person and in the group as a whole. If time is short, you can pray (or ask if one person would volunteer to pray).

LESSON 3: HOW DO WE DO CHRISTIAN COMMUNITY?

LESSON OVERVIEW

I. BIG IDEA	Read (or ask a volunteer to read) the Big Idea aloud (2 min)
II. BIBLE CONVERSATION	Read and talk about the passages (10 min)
III. ARTICLE	Read "How Do We Do Christian Community?" together (10 min)
IV. DISCUSSION	Process the concepts together (15 min)
V. EXERCISE	Apply the concepts using the "Faith Expressing Itself Through Love" exercise (15-20 min)
VI. WRAP-UP	Share final thoughts and pray (5 min)

BIBLE CONVERSATION *(10 min)*

The two passages in this lesson will begin to give the group an idea of what Christian community should be like and how it is drastically different from the self-centered way we relate to people in our flesh. In Luke 6:32–36 Jesus describes how people commonly interact with one another—loving just those who love them. But Jesus calls his followers to extend love and mercy even to their enemies. In Acts 2:42–45 we see believers living in close community—learning, eating, and praying together and sharing their possessions with one another. What characterizes Jesus's followers so that they can live in this countercultural way? Faith in Christ that expresses itself in love for others (Galatians 5:6).

SETUP   We are again going to read two passages this week, one from the Gospel of Luke and one from Acts. These passages will show us a little bit of what a community that is centered on the gospel of Jesus looks like.

READ AND ASK *First reading: Have someone read Luke 6:32–36 aloud. Then answer the questions.*

Second reading: Have someone read Acts 2:42–45 aloud. Then answer the questions.

TRANSITION TO ARTICLE In the Bible passages we read, we heard Jesus's teaching about how to love others, and we saw how early followers of Jesus put their love into action. The article we're about to read will take a closer look at the loving relationships that grow out of faith in Jesus. Let's dig in.

ARTICLE (10 min)

READ THE ARTICLE TOGETHER *Ask the group to turn to the article "How Do We Do Christian Community?" and read it aloud together, taking turns at the paragraph breaks.*

DISCUSSION (15 min)

Read each discussion question aloud, and have participants discuss it.

TRANSITION TO EXERCISE We've seen how relationships that are centered on God are different from relationships that are centered on self. This week's exercise will help us think about how we can love one another.

EXERCISE (15–20 min)

SETUP *Read the introduction (or explain it in your own words), and go over the instructions for the exercise.*

DO THE EXERCISE *This exercise involves both group time and individual reflection. Work through the group parts together, and for the reflection sections, give participants a few minutes to answer the questions on their own.*

TRANSITION TO WRAP-UP   Thank you for reflecting and sharing your thoughts! Before we close, does anyone have any more questions or comments?

WRAP-UP *(5 min)*

Pray together, asking that with the help of the Holy Spirit, everyone in the group would grow in understanding "faith expressing itself through love" and see it in their lives more and more.

LESSON 4: A GRACE-FILLED COMMUNITY

LESSON OVERVIEW

I. BIG IDEA — Read (or ask a volunteer to read) the Big Idea aloud (2 min)

II. BIBLE CONVERSATION — Read and talk about the passages (10 min)

III. ARTICLE — Read "A Grace-Filled Community" together (10 min)

IV. DISCUSSION — Process the concepts together (15 min)

V. EXERCISE — Apply the concepts using the "Growing in Grace" exercise (15 min)

VI. WRAP-UP — Share final thoughts and pray (5 min)

BIBLE CONVERSATION *(10 min)*

*This week's passages introduce **grace**. In Luke 7:36–47 we see a specific instance of grace. We meet a woman who understands that she has sinned and knows she needs forgiveness, and we see the kind grace of Jesus, who forgives her sins and accepts her worship. In contrast, Simon the Pharisee judges the woman because he cannot see his own sin and need for grace. The verses from Titus give us the big picture of grace. All humans were doomed because of their disobedience, and in his loving-kindness God gave us Jesus to be our Savior and the Holy Spirit to give us rebirth into a new life.*

SETUP   Our passages this week come from the Gospel of Luke and Paul's letter to Titus. Both of these passages have something to tell us about **grace**. As we read the story in Luke, bear in mind that a Pharisee was a very respected religious leader back in Jesus's time.

READ AND ASK   *First reading: Have someone read Luke 7:36–47 aloud. Then answer the questions.*

Second reading: Have someone read Titus 3:3–8 aloud. Then answer the questions.

TRANSITION TO ARTICLE   In the Bible passages we read, we saw how beautiful God's grace is in Jesus. The article we're going to read next talks about how we can live in the freedom that grace brings. Let's turn to that now.

ARTICLE *(10 min)*

READ THE ARTICLE TOGETHER   *Ask the group to turn to the article "A Grace-Filled Community" and read it aloud together, taking turns at the paragraph breaks.*

DISCUSSION *(15 min)*

Read each discussion question aloud, and have participants discuss it.

TRANSITION TO EXERCISE   We just read about how pride and fear can get in the way of experiencing grace and how we need the Holy Spirit to work in us. In this exercise we will spend some time looking at ways the Holy Spirit can change us.

EXERCISE *(15 min)*

SETUP   *Read the introduction (or explain it in your own words), and go over the instructions for the exercise.*

DO THE EXERCISE   *Give participants several minutes to work through the chart on their own.*

SHARE   *Once participants have worked through the chart, give them the opportunity to share if they wish.*

TRANSITION TO WRAP-UP   Thank you for working through this exercise, and thanks for sharing! We're about to wrap up, but does anyone have any more questions or comments?

WRAP-UP *(5 min)*

Pray together, asking the Holy Spirit to help everyone in the group feel loved and secure in the grace God has given them and to help them extend grace to others.

LESSON 5: A HUMBLE COMMUNITY

LESSON OVERVIEW

I. BIG IDEA	Read (or ask a volunteer to read) the Big Idea aloud (2 min)
II. BIBLE CONVERSATION	Read and talk about the passage (10 min)
III. ARTICLE	Read "Humility and Community" together (10 min)
IV. DISCUSSION	Process the concepts together (15 min)
V. EXERCISE	Apply the concepts using the "Pride and Prejudice" exercise (15 min)
VI. WRAP-UP	Share final thoughts and pray (5 min)

BIBLE CONVERSATION *(10 min)*

Mark 10:35–45 is a study in humility—and its opposite. James and John are seeking glory for themselves, and the reaction of the other disciples shows that glory isn't far from their minds either. They are thinking the way the world thinks, wanting what the world says we should want. But Jesus's way is completely different: Greatness lies in humble service. This is how Jesus himself lived his life on earth. As the Son of Man, Jesus is worthy of praise (Daniel 7:13–14), but he lived among us in humility, not seeking to be served, but serving and giving up his life for others.

SETUP   Today we're going to read a conversation between Jesus and his disciples from the Gospel of Mark. Jesus and his disciples have different views of what it means to be great.

READ AND ASK   *Have someone read Mark 10:35–45 aloud. Then answer the questions.*

TRANSITION TO ARTICLE This conversation with Jesus shows us that the key to true greatness is humble service. So how does that play out in community? Let's read the article to see.

ARTICLE *(10 min)*

READ THE ARTICLE TOGETHER *Ask the group to turn to the article "Humility and Community" and read it aloud together, taking turns at the paragraph breaks.*

DISCUSSION *(15 min)*

Read each discussion question aloud, and have participants discuss it.

TRANSITION TO EXERCISE The article talked about how the gospel of grace moves us from being prideful "consumers" to being humble servants. This exercise will get us thinking about what it would look like for us as individuals and as a group to move from pride to humility.

EXERCISE *(15 min)*

SETUP *Read the introduction (or explain it in your own words).*

DO THE EXERCISE *Give participants several minutes to work through the checklist and answer the questions in Part 1. Then do Part 2 together.*

TRANSITION TO WRAP-UP Thank you for doing this exercise. We're about to wrap up, but are there any more questions or comments?

WRAP-UP *(5 min)*

Pray together, asking the Holy Spirit to help everyone in the group gain freedom from prideful self-concern and grow in humility and service to others.

LESSON 6: HONEST RELATIONSHIPS

LESSON OVERVIEW

I. BIG IDEA	Read (or ask a volunteer to read) the Big Idea aloud (2 min)
II. BIBLE CONVERSATION	Read and talk about the passages (10 min)
III. ARTICLE	Read "Honest Relationships" together (10 min)
IV. DISCUSSION	Process the concepts together (15 min)
V. EXERCISE	Apply the concepts using the "Speaking the Truth in Love" exercise (15 min)
VI. WRAP-UP	Share final thoughts and pray (5 min)

BIBLE CONVERSATION *(10 min)*

When we are in Christ, our life looks different: It starts to reflect the character of the One we follow. Our first passage, 1 John 1:5–9, calls this way of living "walking in the light." Our second passage, Ephesians 4:15, 25–32, gives us some specifics of what it looks like to live in the light. One of the things Paul highlights in these verses is the importance of honesty. He describes believers as "speaking the truth in love," and he encourages us to "put off falsehood and speak truthfully to your neighbor" (verses 15, 25).

SETUP *Before reading each passage, read the brief introduction to it.*

READ AND ASK *First reading: Have someone read 1 John 1:5–9 aloud. Then answer the questions.*

Second reading: Have someone read Ephesians 4:15, 25–32 aloud. Then answer the question.

TRANSITION TO ARTICLE Both of the passages we looked at high-lighted *truth*. We're about to read an article that focuses on two kinds of truthfulness: being honest about ourselves and being honest with others. Let's read to find out more.

ARTICLE *(10 min)*

READ THE ARTICLE TOGETHER *Ask the group to turn to the article "Honest Relationships" and read it aloud together, taking turns at the paragraph breaks.*

DISCUSSION *(15 min)*

Read each discussion question aloud, and have participants discuss it.

TRANSITION TO EXERCISE The article reminds us that because of the grace of the gospel, we can be honest about ourselves and honest with others. Now we're going to do an exercise to help us identify where we struggle with being truthful and how the gospel can free us.

EXERCISE *(15 min)*

SETUP *Read the introduction (or explain it in your own words), and go over the instructions for the exercise.*

DO THE EXERCISE *Give participants several minutes to work through the questions on their own.*

SHARE *Once participants have worked through the questions, give them the opportunity to share if they wish.*

TRANSITION TO WRAP-UP Thanks for working through these questions. And thanks for sharing. Does anyone have any more questions or comments before we wrap up?

WRAP-UP *(5 min)*

Pray together, asking the Holy Spirit to help us remember the truths we have learned so that we will grow in being honest with one another in a loving, humble way.

LESSON 7: A JOYFUL COMMUNITY

LESSON OVERVIEW

I. BIG IDEA	Read (or ask a volunteer to read) the Big Idea aloud (2 min)
II. BIBLE CONVERSATION	Read and talk about the passages (10 min)
III. ARTICLE	Read "A Joyful Community" together (10 min)
IV. DISCUSSION	Process the concepts together (15 min)
V. EXERCISE	Apply the concepts using the "Happiness Killers" exercise (15 min)
VI. WRAP-UP	Share final thoughts and pray (5 min)

BIBLE CONVERSATION *(10 min)*

This week the group will be reading three very short passages. The first is a one-verse parable about joy. The next two little passages reassure us that God himself is at work in us to sanctify us, to make us more and more like him.

SETUP   *Before reading each passage, read the brief introduction to it.*

READ AND ASK   *First reading: Have someone read Matthew 13:44 aloud. Then answer the questions.*

Second reading: Have someone read 1 Thessalonians 5:23–24 and 2 Corinthians 3:17–18 aloud. Then answer the questions.

TRANSITION TO ARTICLE   The first passage we read was about joy, and the other two were about sanctification. Now we're going to read an article that will help us see how misunderstanding sanctification can sap our joy.

ARTICLE *(10 min)*

`READ THE ARTICLE TOGETHER`   *Ask the group to turn to the article "A Joyful Community" and read it aloud together, taking turns at the paragraph breaks.*

DISCUSSION *(15 min)*

Read each discussion question aloud, and have participants discuss it.

`TRANSITION TO EXERCISE`   The article discussed how we can be joyful when we remember that our justification is *secure*. The exercise that we are turning to now will help us identify things that might be robbing us of our joy.

EXERCISE *(15 min)*

`SETUP`   *Read the introduction (or explain it in your own words), and go over the instructions for the exercise.*

`DO THE EXERCISE`   *Give participants a few minutes to work through the checklist on their own.*

`SHARE`   *Once participants have finished the checklist, discuss the sharing questions together.*

`TRANSITION TO WRAP-UP`   Thanks for this discussion. Before we finish, does anyone have any more questions or comments?

WRAP-UP *(5 min)*

Pray together, asking the Holy Spirit to help us cling to the truth that we have been justified by faith and to fill us with joy because of this gracious gift.

LESSON 8: A COMMUNITY ON A MISSION

LESSON OVERVIEW

I. BIG IDEA	Read (or ask a volunteer to read) the Big Idea aloud (2 min)
II. BIBLE CONVERSATION	Read and talk about the passage (10 min)
III. ARTICLE	Read "A Missional Community" together (10 min)
IV. DISCUSSION	Process the concepts together (15 min)
V. EXERCISE	Apply the concepts using the "Living on Mission" exercise (15–20 min)
VI. WRAP-UP	Share final thoughts and pray (5 min)

BIBLE CONVERSATION *(10 min)*

The passage for this lesson, 2 Corinthians 5:14–20, reflects the urgency Paul felt about sharing "the message of reconciliation" as one of "Christ's ambassadors" (verses 19–20). Paul certainly had a unique experience of being called to faith in Jesus, and he had a clear call to spread the good news of Jesus around the Roman Empire. We may not have been blinded by a heavenly light, but we too—all of us who have put our faith in Jesus—are called to be ambassadors, loving people around us (wherever we find ourselves) and sharing with them the good news that through Jesus we can be reconciled with God.

SETUP *Before reading the passage, read the brief introduction to it.*

READ AND ASK *Have someone read 2 Corinthians 5:14–20 aloud. Then answer the questions.*

TRANSITION TO ARTICLE The verses we just read talked about how God sent Jesus to reconcile people to himself. Let's turn to the article to read about how we can be part of God's mission to rescue people and bring them into his family.

ARTICLE *(10 min)*

READ THE ARTICLE TOGETHER *Ask the group to turn to the article "A Missional Community" and read it aloud together, taking turns at the paragraph breaks.*

DISCUSSION *(15 min)*

Read each discussion question aloud, and have participants discuss it.

TRANSITION TO EXERCISE The article discussed how we can be part of what God is doing in the world by moving toward other people. This exercise will help us think about ways we can be ambassadors right where God has put us.

EXERCISE *(15-20 min)*

SETUP *Read the introduction (or explain it in your own words), and go over the instructions for the exercise.*

DO THE EXERCISE *Give participants several minutes to work through the questions on their own.*

SHARE *Once participants have finished the questions, take a few minutes to let participants share some of the ideas they came up with.*

TRANSITION TO WRAP-UP Thank you for your participation today, and thanks for all the thinking and praying and discussing you've done over the last several weeks! We're about to close in prayer, but does anyone have any more questions or comments?

WRAP-UP *(5 min)*

Pray together, asking the Holy Spirit to give members of the group hearts that want to move toward people and opportunities to do so. Pray that members of the group would encourage one another as they seek to be on mission.

ENDNOTES

1. The "grey town" is based on C. S. Lewis's depiction of hell in *The Great Divorce* (New York: Collier Books, 1946), 11–19.

2. Lewis, *Great Divorce*, 19.

3. Freddie deBoer, "Some Reasons Why Smartphones Might Make Adolescents Anxious and Depressed," Freddie DeBoer, March 7, 2023, https://freddiedeboer.substack.com/p/some-reasons-why-smartphones -might.

4. Kathryn Spink, *Mother Teresa: A Complete Authorized Biography* (New York: HarperCollins, 1997), 18–21.

5. Brennan Manning, *Abba's Child* (NavPress, 2002), 31.

6. In his book *Happiness* (Tyndale House Publishers, 2024), Randy Alcorn shows that in the Bible, "joy" and "happiness" are used synonymously, along with other words like "gladness," "blessed," and "delight."

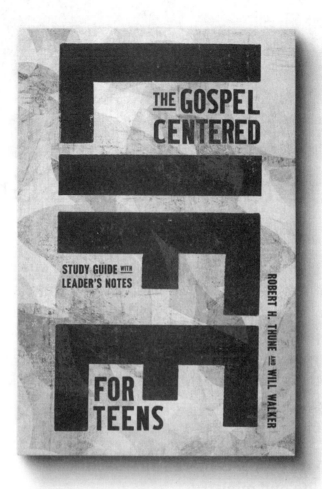

THE GOSPEL-CENTERED LIFE FOR TEENS

Robert H. Thune and Will Walker

The Gospel-Centered Life for Teens is a 9-week curriculum designed to help young adults explore how the gospel shapes every part of their lives. Each lesson is crafted to spark meaningful conversation, challenge surface-level thinking, and draw students into a deeper relationship with Jesus. Perfect for youth groups, Sunday schools, and campus ministries, this study equips teens to grow spiritually and live out their faith with authenticity and purpose.

NEW GROWTH PRESS

newgrowthpress.com

mission
propelled by God's Grace

Go and grow with us.

Since 1983, Serge has been helping individuals and churches engage in global mission. From short-term trips to long-term missions – we want to see the power of God's grace transform your own life and motivate and sustain you to move into the lives of others – particularly those who do not yet know Jesus.

As a sending agency we:

- **Take a gospel-centered approach to life and ministry**
- **Provide proactive Missionary Care**
- **Practice incarnational ministry**
- **Believe God works in our weakness**

Visit us online at:
serge.org/missions

Grace at the Fray

Gospel Renewal

Renewal → Mission

fuels mission

Serge is...

As an international missions agency, we realize we need the grace of the gospel in our own lives, even as we take the message of God's grace to others. Our work consists of helping people experience ongoing *gospel renewal* and equipping them to move outward into *mission*.

We seek to foster this transformation in ministry leaders, churches, and all believers around the world.

Visit us online at:
serge.org

MISSIONS | MENTORING | RESOURCES

Grace at the Fray

resources

for continued spiritual growth

We never outgrow our need for the gospel.

No matter where you are on your Christian journey, Serge resources help you live out the gospel in every part of your life and encourage the same growth in others. Whether you are a church leader, actively engaged in ministry, or just seeking to go deeper in your relationship with God - we have resources that can help.

- **Books and Studies**
- **Discipleship and Training**
- **Grace-Centered Teaching Events**
- **Webinars**
- **Podcast**

Visit us online at:
serge.org/renewal

Grace at the Fray